AF326644

# About Our Featured Author

**Ginger King**, known as *The Beauty Shark*, is an award-winning cosmetic chemist, entrepreneur, and speaker whose journey embodies resilience, vision, and bold reinvention. Born in Taiwan and raised by her mother and grandmother after losing her father as an infant, Ginger came to America as a teenager with little more than determination and a dream.

She went from analyzing pineapples at Dole Foods to formulating multimillion-dollar beauty products, proving that every setback can become a stepping stone. Today, she is the founder of **Grace Kingdom Beauty,** a consulting firm creating shelf-ready brands from concept to launch, and **FanLoveBeauty**, a clean vegan line inspired by her mentor Daymond John of *Shark Tank*.

Crowned "The Queen of Cosmetic Chemistry" by *Elle* magazine, Ginger has been quoted in over 40 publications, featured on *Forbes, Inc.,* and *Success Magazine*, and named one of *Success Magazine's Top 50 Women of Influence.* She is also a certified **10X Business Coach** trained by Grant Cardone—who calls her proof of what's possible when you live the 10X Rule.

From underdog to industry icon, Ginger's life is proof that no matter where you start, you can create beauty, business, and a legacy that lasts.

# Praise

Ginger King lives the 10X Rule. Immigrant. Hustler. Beauty mogul. This book shows what's possible when you go all-in.
—GRANT CARDONE, CEO of Cardone Enterprises,
NYT Bestselling Author of The 10X Rule

Ginger King is the real deal. She's got that relentless hustle, a no-excuses attitude, and a gift for turning setbacks into stepping stones. Her journey from an underdog to an industry powerhouse is proof that when you mix passion with perseverance, anything is possible. This book isn't just a story—it's a blueprint for anyone who wants to turn their dream into a legacy. I've watched Ginger put in the work, and I'm proud to call her a friend and a force in the world of beauty and business.
—Daymond John, founder of FUBU, star of Shark Tank

This book is a must-read for any entrepreneur starting a business. Ginger King shows you the grit, hustle and heart it takes to go from nothing to something.
—BARBARA CORCORAN, Founder, The Corcoran Group,
Shark on Shark Tank

Ginger King's journey is proof that when you lead with service, faith, and fierce determination, success is inevitable. This book is a guide for anyone who's been underestimated and still chose to show up, give more, and grow into greatness. It's not just about beauty—it's about becoming the best version of yourself.

—David Meltzer, Chairman of The Napoleon Hill Institute

This book is more than a memoir—it's a masterclass in resilience, reinvention, and what it really takes to build a beauty legacy from the ground up. Ginger King doesn't just talk about the industry—she's lived every aspect of it, from lab bench to boardroom. A must-read for any founder who's serious about building a brand with brains, backbone, and heart.

—Kelly Kovack, Founder and CEO of BeautyMatter

STAND ON THE SHOULDERS™
*of*
TOP-PRODUCING INDUSTRY
# GIANTS

# STAND ON THE SHOULDERS™
*of*
## TOP-PRODUCING INDUSTRY
# GIANTS
## FEATURING

**13 UNIQUE INDIVIDUALS ALL SHARING THEIR PERSONAL JOURNEYS OF HOW THEY TURNED THEIR LIVES AROUND AND ACHIEVED SUCCESS.**

Ginger King

Johnny Wimbrey

Meeshie Lee

Kate Stone
and Zac Gordon

Ryan Hill

Brenda Petrillo

Cary Clayborn

Netasha Reed

Ndidi Musa, M.D

Col. Tammy S. Hinskton

Brad Hammond

Stan Lewis

Michael Chiasson

Published by Wimbrey Training Systems 550 Reserve Street, Suite 190 Southlake, Texas 76092

Printed in the United States of America



ISBN 978-1-971010-17-5

# Dedication

*This book is dedicated to my family—my mother Ava, my husband Ronald, and my son Martin—who are my everything.*

*And to my mentors, whose wisdom and guidance I deeply cherish, especially Grant Cardone and Daymond John, who continue to inspire me to dream bigger and bolder.*

# Contents

# CONTENTS

# Introduction

**An Introduction to**
**The Stand on the Shoulders of Giants™ Series**

This powerful new hardcover series is inspired by the words Sir Isaac Newton made famous: *If I have seen further, it is by standing on the shoulders of giants.*

The first three books in the series are:

- *Stand on the Shoulders of Multi-Million-Producing Giants*
- *Stand on the Shoulders of Top-Producing Giants*
- *Stand on the Shoulders of Mindset Mastery Coaching Giants*

There was a time in my life when I was expected to fail. By the grace of God, I succeeded because I was able to stand on the shoulders of giants. Now it's my turn to pass on the quantum boost I received. The authors contributing to the *Stand on the Shoulders of Giants* series are modern-day giants and elite leaders, and sharing their knowledge is vital to my life's work.

My guidelines for publishing this extraordinary hardcover series were simple but compelling: I knew it was vital to introduce you to modern giants—men and women of character and authenticity who thrive despite the world of compromise in which we live. The authors aren't perfect. They haven't lived flawless lives, nor have I. But as you turn the pages of each book in the *Stand on the Shoulders of Giants* series, you'll discover the authors' exceptional principles and character, their generosity of spirit, their brilliance. *Their truth.*

Each book in our guaranteed best-selling series is unique, and each author is chosen carefully for their strong story and character. You will find genuine connections and authentic voices that resonate with you.

In today's social media-driven culture, we are witnessing a shift unlike any other in human history. For the first time since the beginning of time, society is elevating people to "giant" stature based on the number of followers they have, the number of views they generate, and how many comments are made on their platforms. We are celebrating *visibility* over *credibility* and confusing *influence* with *wisdom*.

I believe in something much deeper—what every ancient tribe understood instinctively when life gets real: **You don't go to the influencers; you go to the elders.** You go to those who have *lived, fallen, and risen again* and have scars that speak louder than any trending soundbite. You go to the ones who carry wisdom for survival—and who can share and inspire.

These are my giants, my elders, whom I invited to be in this series.

They are elders in their achievements, experience, character, wisdom, and leadership. Though relatively young, they write not from a platform of perfection, but from a foundation of truth. Our authors are qualified at the highest elite levels—because *they've been there; they've done that*. And they excelled.

Now they offer their shoulders to you, to boost you to a better view of your path ahead.

As we know all too well, our paths aren't always smooth. Sir Winston Churchill perfectly captured the heartbeat of the *Stand on the Shoulders of Giants* series when he said:

*If you're going through hell, keep going.*

Every one of the modern-day giants who authors a chapter in our series keeps going on the path of success—through setbacks, shame, failure, heartbreak, loss, rejection, betrayal, and pressure that would break most people. They don't stop. And because they don't, they have more than just massive success—they have substance and character.

When you connect with modern giants and they elevate your thinking, extraordinary things begin to happen. Your mind expands, your options and possibilities broaden, you challenge your limitations, and you start living your life without the limitations that have held you back. You see better and further.

I challenge you: Make a commitment to each title in our powerful *Stand on the Shoulders of Giants* series and find the giants who help you see further. Don't skim the chapters. Don't cherry-pick. Read every story—from front to back. Take your time. Sit with their stories and listen to their voices. Take what they offer and see further down the road.

Awaken the giant within you!

—*Johnny Wimbrey, Ph.D.*

# Foreword

'm honored to bring you the second book in the best-selling *On the Shoulders of Giants*™ series. Twelve of the most impressive professionals and business people in the United States and Canada have joined me to write *Stand on the Shoulders of Top-Producing Industry Giants.*

Each of the people who joined me to write a chapter in this book was chosen by me after multiple interviews and my team's careful consideration of what they have to offer you. Every author is a highly sought-after leader, a top-level producer in entrepreneurship or sales, or a visionary, high-performance founder. I know their habits, strengths, and weaknesses.

My co-authors are at different stages of their careers, but you will notice we all have one important thing in common: *We look forward to the future.* We maintain a far-sighted view of our opportunities and possibilities while we build our legacies.

We are elite-level leaders with empire mindsets. We are not limited by our pasts. Without shame or excuses, we share our mistakes, what we're most proud of, and which ethical and moral standards guide us. Many of us talk about our deep faith and how it has helped us. We discuss our attitude, making room for philanthropy, and making the most of second (or third, or fourth) chances. We have much to offer you.

As in all the titles within the *Stand on the Shoulders of Giants* series, our integrity and character are the heart of this powerful book. We realize their importance to our success. This book is about building the character and resilience you need to succeed.

"Standing on the shoulders of giants" is a metaphor almost 1,000 years old; it means having the opportunity to build on the wisdom and truths of others who've gone before you. The genius Isaac Newton made the phrase famous when he wrote, "If I have seen further, it is by standing on the shoulders of giants."

In *Stand on the Shoulders of Top-Producing Industry Giants*, we offer you the unprecedented opportunity to stand on our shoulders, share our wisdom, see your future more clearly, and reach it sooner.

***Johnny Wimbrey, Ph.D.***

# Resilience and Vision Can Take You Far

GINGER KING

**M**y father and I never got to know one another because he passed away when I was only three months old. That tragedy could have been the beginning of a story about a little girl who never grew up to do big things, but instead, my mother made sure I had every opportunity to achieve greatness.

My mother set a strong example for me. She ran the first boutique selling Shiseido Luxury Skin Care in Taiwan and was the second woman in the country to get a driver's license. My grandmother stepped in to help raise me while my mother worked. Although I did not have a father, the strength of my mother and grandmother surrounded me.

My mother worked very hard to open her own business and made sure it received proper attention. My mom understood the power of publicity. For example, Miss Japan performed the ribbon-cutting ceremony for her Shiseido boutique.

One of my earliest memories is hiding under a table at her boutique. When I think back, I can still smell the lemon scent infused in her skin care products and feel the tablecloth against my skin. It was an excellent hideout for me to listen and learn and sow the seeds for my beauty entrepreneurial journey.

I wasn't into skin care yet; I was just a kid. When I started school, makeup still wasn't interesting to me because we were not allowed to wear it—our focus was our studies, not vanity. We wore uniforms every day, too.

The first part of our school days began at 8 a.m. and ended at 5 p.m. In the evening, we attended additional CRAM classes for supplementary learning. Without those evening classes, my grades would have been even lower than they were. In our regular classes, teachers ignored students who did not show up for CRAM classes, viewing them as unserious and unpromising.

I attended classes six days a week. At that time, children in Taiwan did not spend Saturday mornings watching cartoons or Saturday afternoons at sports events. We spent our time studying. That's just the way it was. None of us ever thought it was unusual or unfair. Sundays were for sleep. With one day of rest, we started all over on Monday.

I still work on weekends. I expect partners and colleagues to be available for work matters on weekends, too. I didn't get to where I am today by taking 48 hours off every week!

In Taiwan, getting into college requires passing entrance exams—one to move from junior high to high school, and another from high school to college. I attended a prestigious all-girls private school where the junior high and senior high were connected. If your grades were good enough, you could move up without taking the entrance exam and even continue to the internationally recognized Sacred Heart College.

I spent four years there—three in junior high and one in senior high. I struggled academically the whole time. I was failing math, home economics, and physical education. In Taiwan, if your grades aren't good, you don't have many options. You are only allowed to pursue a career within the range of your academic grades. There was no way my grades would enable me to pursue anything other than a life of mediocrity, and I knew I was capable and deserved more than what some test scores reflected. That pressure led to a big decision.

My mother's siblings were already in America. We both understood that staying in Taiwan meant I would not have a future. My mother did not hesitate to leave her business and life behind to bring me to America. We joined my uncle in Sugarland, Texas. Once there, my mom started taking babysitting jobs, and I began my sophomore year of American high school.

I attended a co-ed public school in a very wealthy neighborhood. The students were mainly rude and arrogant. No one in my school spoke Chinese, but they were not at all impressed that I knew English. Instead, other students bullied me for my accent. People in California could understand my English, but in that part of Texas, with its own strong accent, they did not.

There is a definite difference in cultures between Taiwan and America. I didn't understand why my tenth-grade American math teacher, who was teaching the same math we learned in first grade at home, got mad at me for correcting her. My classmates didn't like it either. It was a very frustrating time for me, but I excelled academically. The standards in America were far below those in Taiwan. My grades were strong, though I felt as if the teachers didn't like me.

The library became my refuge. Studying after school became a pleasure when it was by choice instead of demand. While other students went to sports or parties, I went to the library. It was there that I found Estée Lauder's biography. Lauder was a very successful American businesswoman. Estée began learning about skincare during her teens through mentorship from her uncle, John Schotz, a chemist who created skin creams.

Estée believed every woman could be beautiful and worked hard to bring quality beauty products to more people. She also created bright marketing ideas, such as giving free samples and gifts with each purchase.

Reading her story ignited something inside me. I was inspired. I wanted to be like her. I read every book I could find on cosmetics. The field was fascinating. That's when I knew I would build a career and be successful in the cosmetic industry. I really wanted to be a makeup artist right out of high school because I saw how makeup can transform people's appearances and level of confidence. I also knew my family expected me to earn a master's degree, at a minimum. In Asian culture, if you don't get a Ph.D., you'd better at least get a Master's. When the cosmetologist school called, my family said "Ginger? Cosmetology School? You got the wrong number!" So, I decided to study chemistry and become a cosmetic chemist.

My SAT essay was all about how I wanted to build a career in cosmetics so I could turn ugly ducklings into swans. I scored high enough to have my choice of colleges. I also knew my family expected me to earn a master's degree, at a minimum.

I was accepted to San Jose State University in California, and it felt like home. There's a large Asian community there, and it was a relief to be back among people with whom I shared commonalities. Our culture was the same. Our language was the same. The extracurricular opportunities were intellectually and personally stimulating.

I found the chemistry teachers to be the most inspiring. That was especially good for me because I always did better in classes with teachers I liked. I went from being the girl who failed chemistry in Taiwan to the young woman whose college chemistry professor asked her to be a Teaching Assistant.

When I was younger, I was obsessed with a Hong Kong pop star, Leslie Cheung, a superstar who spoke Cantonese. I was so infatuated with him that I even learned to speak Cantonese so that I could communicate with him. That turned out to be helpful for me later.

I met my future husband in my junior year of college at a birthday party hosted by a mutual friend. I almost didn't go because I had to study for an exam, but a friend of mine would not stop telling me to "Go, go, go! You will meet your own 'Leslie Cheung' there!" That friend clearly knew me well. It worked, and I went.

The dance I shared with the man I met there turned into a romantic relationship, and I married him. My husband, Ronald, is five years older than I am. He is Cantonese, from Hong Kong, and it was important to him that anyone he dated spoke Cantonese. Thank you for the inspiration, Leslie Cheung!

While I enjoyed college chemistry, the curriculum did not include anything about making cosmetics. So, I began experimenting in my dorm room. I found perfume and cosmetic formulas in library books. I'd look up the addresses for chemical companies, write to them asking for free samples of raw materials, and they'd send them. I doubt it would be so easy today with liability issues. But it worked for me then.

> Legacy isn't inherited; it's created.

Because floral fragrances were my focus, my dorm room always had a floral scent. I gave a lot of what I produced to my fragrance-loving mother.

A chemistry degree, I knew, would not in itself be enough to build a career on. I initially minored in business and went on to earn an MBA in marketing.

A lot of marketing is different today, of course, but the core principles are the same. I still remember valuable information from classes like Pricing Theories and Sales Management. Outside of class, I discovered inspirational and motivational books by authors like Brian Tracy, as well as books on mastering the art of selling by Tom Hopkins. Those books instilled the entrepreneurship spirit in me.

With college behind me, it was time to find my first full-time job. I could not wait to begin my journey to my cosmetic career—but I needed to be patient. The cosmetics industry is not an easy one to break into.

I sent out 100 resumes. I had interviewed with some cosmetics companies, but I quickly realized no one would hire me without specific cosmetic industry experience. It's the same frustrating part of the process so many new college graduates go through: We cannot get hired without experience, but we cannot get experience without being hired! But I was determined to find my way, so I improvised.

I began as a temp at Dole Foods. It is an American company, but all its employees with doctorates were American-born Chinese. There I was again welcomed and felt comfortable. My job was to analyze vitamin C in pineapple juice and salads. The work gave me experience with vitamin C, which is an ingredient in many cosmetics.

I worked full-time at Dole during the day and kept the part-time evening job I had started in college in fragrance sales. I loved that job. When other salespeople stammered to respond to customers asking why some products were so expensive, I made them laugh by replying, "Because you don't want to smell cheap!" My sales numbers soared.

My opportunity to move into the makeup department arrived when someone left, and the manager really needed to fill the spot. She knew I didn't have experience as a makeup artist. She also knew I was passionate about cosmetics, had a natural gift working with customers, and my work ethic was solid. So, she gave me the position.

It was a quiet section of the store, which meant I had no one to practice or demonstrate my makeup skills on. Once again, I improvised. I grabbed the blank cardboard pieces and began applying makeup on pretend faces. That way, when people came to my counter, I could show them my art, and they could imagine themselves as my canvas. It was fun for me. It also translated into higher sales numbers as customers responded to the opportunity to engage with me and be my models.

I worked at that high-end makeup counter for two months. I was grateful for that experience, but in my heart, I still wanted to work at Estée Lauder. When I saw an opening at the Macy's department store, I pounced.

Macy's demanded verifiable experience to consider hiring someone. I went right in and wowed them with my stories of all the people I helped during my two months at the makeup counter. I shared how I dedicated a college essay to how to beautify the world with Estée Lauder Fragrances, making sure to point out I got an A+ on that essay. I poured out my passion to them, and they were impressed. Then, I became their top salesperson. The expectation there was that we had to sell three products to each customer. If you sold one product at a time, their theory was that you were just a vending machine.

So, when a customer comes in for a lipstick, for example, we should also sell them a lip pencil and a blush. Of course, I didn't tell them I had to sell three products. I just gave them the whole experience from head to toe, finishing them with the fragrance. I pampered them. One time, I had a pair of twins sit down at my counter. By the time I finished with one of them, the other one was so impressed she bought everything her sister did. That was a $600 sale, which would be around $2,500 today.

The long days didn't bother me. If you love what you're doing, it's fun. And I loved retail. I still do, really. My time in retail also gives me an edge that many do not have. Those who work their way up through corporate channels and skip working directly with customers often overlook what really drives a consumer to buy their product.

For instance, in sales, you need to calm people down. They tend to get nervous about buying a big-ticket item. But if you can joke around with them, they relax, they connect with you, and they trust you. I had one customer who bought all his fragrances from another department store. He somehow wound up at my counter after that. I spent some time showing him our products and joking around with him. He returned all the products to that store and then repurchased them from me.

I have never sold a product I don't believe in. I am not tricking anyone into buying from me so that I can make a commission. That's the difference between me and the salesperson at the other store, who had to return $300 to my new customer.

I didn't *need* that retail job. I made very good money as a chemist at Dole Foods. So, I had fun with it, and I told people exactly what I thought, even if it meant selling fewer products to them.

If they were considering buying two different creams that did the same thing, I'd tell them they only needed one. Many desperate commission-based employees would not do that. However, besides being the right thing to do, it usually resulted in *more* sales because people appreciated my honesty and trusted me to provide them with sound advice.

People often ask me for advice about how to break into an industry or niche they are passionate about. They see me now, running my own company, with friends like Daymond John, helping people as a Grant Cardone Certified 10X Business Coach, and wanting to know how they can build success and relationships like that. My advice to them is simple:

*Find a way.*

I wanted to be a makeup artist, and I didn't look at any position as too small or beneath me when I set out to achieve that. My energy and work ethic allowed me to create my own opportunity to become a makeup artist at Macy's.

I got my chemistry degree to satisfy my family's expectations and discovered my love for cosmetic chemistry. I didn't just wake up one morning with powerful, successful friends and my own company, I am proud of. I *worked* on those things. I added value to other people. I proved I can deliver. I started small and built on every experience I had.

You can, too.

What do you like? What are you passionate about? There must be some corner of that industry you can get into. Get your foot in the door, no matter how—even if it's an unpaid job—and make a name for yourself.

I mentor quite a few young people. Many of them have a stuck-up attitude: "I'm sure I can get a *paid* job." And I sigh and think, "Okay, then you keep looking. Good luck."

It's not because no one ever finds a paying job in the area they love. But for those highly competitive disciplines or careers, the path is never a direct line. It's always the person who is willing to do whatever it takes, work the jobs on the fringe of that industry, gain experience, build a reputation, and put in the time to outperform those who are unwilling to do any of that.

My husband has always known I am an ambitious woman. I made it very clear to him from the beginning of our relationship that I planned to move to New York City, the birthplace of Estée Lauder, and build success there. Before I married him, he agreed to move with me.

> " It was a start, and a start is all I ever needed. "

Knowing we would one day move across the country made finding a cosmetic chemist job seem easy. It was time for me to transition into a career in the field of cosmetic chemistry, and those jobs were five hours away from where we lived at the time.

I knocked on door after door in Los Angeles. I didn't have an appointment with anyone. I just walked in, introduced myself, explained what I do, and why they should hire me. At least that's what I did to the few people who agreed to meet with me. Most of the companies I approached didn't even give me that opportunity.

My husband and I never wasted money and saved a good portion of our salaries. When the door that finally opened for me offered me a job at $30,000 below my current salary, I took it. It was a start, and a start is all I ever needed.

That cosmetics company was very different from where I'd just worked.

I was the only chemist there with a degree. The lower-salaried, lower-skilled, lower-motivated staff did not exactly welcome an ambitious, educated, hard-charging Asian woman into their world.

But I didn't care. I wasn't there to make friends. I was there to work. My plans were to use that opportunity to build my resume and then find a better place to work.

I wrote a whole new standard operating procedure for that company, got the resume enhancement, went to that company's competitor, and they hired me on the spot.

My new boss had a reputation for being a tyrant in the beauty industry. He told his employees he'd put a bed in the lab for us so we could take naps and then work through the night. He would regularly walk in and drop massive amounts of work on us. Some people may have disliked it, but I persevered.

He allowed me to exercise my marketing skills, which I loved doing. I wrote stories for every product I sold, further developing my marketing skills while helping with the company's sales figures.

My career path continued evolving. After working at two high-pressure cosmetic manufacturing companies, I found myself in a company with a completely different environment, more relaxed and slower paced. I quickly became bored.

That changed around Christmas when the owner's son approached me with an idea. He coached a swimming team, and his swimmers were constantly frustrated with their hair after practice. They'd layer on gel and hairspray to get it to spike again, and their hair always looked like a mess. He asked if I could come up with something better.

I jumped at the chance. I drew on my knowledge of sunscreen technology—specifically, water resistance—and incorporated it into a regular cream gel formula. The result was the first water-resistant hair styling glue. The swimmers loved it, and it quickly caught on with other kids, too. They didn't even have to brush their hair the next morning. It just stayed in place. That product became my claim to fame. It turned into a multimillion-dollar success.

But success attracts imitation. Nine other companies tried to copy my formula. I could tell exactly who copied me because I had included specific signature ingredients. The most accurate copy came from *Got2B Spiking Glue*, which, ironically, was made by the company that now owns the company I worked for at the time. So technically, they own my formula.

It was both flattering and frustrating. I didn't get royalties. I didn't get a patent. But at least I made a name for myself in the industry. And now people were knocking on my door. It was another pivotal moment in my life. That experience taught me a critical lesson: innovation isn't enough without marketing and business knowledge. That's when I decided to pursue my MBA.

It was a lot of work, but I knew I needed a deeper understanding of the business side of beauty if I ever wanted to build something of my own.

The day finally came when one of the largest cosmetic companies in the country offered me a job. Even better, the company was heavily staffed with people who spoke Chinese. The company was about 40 miles north of New York City. I worked hard, made a positive impression, and always kept an eye out for growth opportunities. During my time there, I focused on hair care before moving up to color cosmetics. Color cosmetics are fun to wear but messy to make. It's not my favorite category; I prefer skin care.

Throughout my entire career, I have never been afraid to start at the bottom, take a pay cut, or move across the country if that's what it took to achieve my long-term goal. You must look not just at today, but at how what you do today will impact you tomorrow or ten years from now. You also must be able to adapt to unexpected life changes.

One of my own significant life changes was having a baby.

I never planned on being a mother. It wasn't something I saw myself doing. But after thirteen years of marriage, two shocking losses unexpectedly hit me. My Cantonese idol, Leslie Cheung, committed suicide. I was still a big fan and still felt some connection to him. Hearing that he'd killed himself really threw me off. When I recovered from that shock, Estée Lauder passed away the same month. The two sudden losses of people I dearly loved made me feel reckless.

"Why not," I told my husband. "We can try one time for a baby."

Nine months later, my son, Martin, was born. I quickly figured out how to balance motherhood and stay focused on my career. I never stayed in any one job longer than I felt it added value to me and my goals. Once I achieved what there was to achieve, I'd move on.

My next move was to join a startup skincare company in New York City. The job was intense. We were 24/7—literally. It was my first experience with a startup, and I grew as an entrepreneur and businesswoman in the fifteen months I spent there. Experiencing how a small team could create something big enough to work with QVC while also working in product development was tough, but I loved every second of it.

It was at my next job where I truly immersed myself in the business side of things, like traveling for presentations, forging connections, and continuously learning. The company is a contract manufacturer, developing and producing products for brand-name cosmetic firms. My job was director of creative business development. Specifically, I was to look at each brand's white space and create a proposal for products. To entice any brand to work with us, we needed to come up with concepts and products proactively and sell to people.

But it wasn't perfect either. After my immediate boss left, I found myself reporting to the president's son, who didn't quite share the same vision on where the company should go. It didn't take long for me to realize it was time to move on.

That's when I began building many personal relationships with big brands. Each time I presented before big players in the industry, I was building my network and my own name recognition.

I then leaped into raw material sales. At first, I wasn't sure it was the right path, but it turned out to be one of the most eye-opening experiences. I sold ingredients to cosmetic companies, including my previous employers, and worked with factories throughout New York. The connections I made were invaluable, and they gave me an even deeper understanding of the industry.

My reputation continued to grow. I co-founded a skincare company, and even though that business did not last, it helped my buzz in the industry grow louder. People began asking me to consult with them. My cash flow was steady, but I knew I was capable of more. That's when I started making even bigger moves.

I had been a fan of Shark Tank for a while, but it wasn't until I saw Daymond John's brilliance in branding that I knew I had to learn more. I started engaging with him on Twitter, and one day, he responded. It was a small interaction, but it set the stage for everything that followed. I didn't hesitate to get myself in front of him. I showed up at events he mentioned and even caught him getting out of a taxi before an interview at Fox News. I was bold, and that boldness caught his attention. Daymond and I started building a relationship, and eventually, he became one of my greatest mentors.

But I didn't make the same mistake as many people do. I didn't ask Daymond to teach me for free. If you want to learn from someone, do not ask or expect them to teach you for free. You need to plug in—to buy what they're offering. I went through Daymond John's whole entrepreneurial academy. It was worth every penny. Daymond was the inspiration for my lip balm. I saw him pull a lip balm out of his pocket and apply it to his lips. Immediately, I told him, "Daymond, if something is so close to you that it's in your pocket and on your lips, it has to be one of *my* products." I then developed my own lip balm with ingredients that are both effective and safe for use, unlike other products.

My mission is to touch a million people's appearances through the products I create. I also want to be known as empowering entrepreneurs in beauty and business. Yes, money is a significant factor of success, but also, how much fulfillment do you feel? Now that I, in turn am coaching others, it's gratifying for me to help my coaching clients solve their problems and build lives they love.

I've learned how to turn what some people view as liabilities into assets. If anyone comments on my accent, I point out it's because I speak more than one language. I am short, so at any event or photo opportunities, you'll see me at the front because I use my height as my asset to get through the crowds.

Today, I am known as Ginger King, the Beauty Shark. I have my own brand, FanLoveBeauty, and my own consulting company, Grace Kingdom Beauty. Additionally, I am a certified 10X Business Coach who trained with Grant Cardone.

Daymond John actually is the reason I became involved with Grant Cardone's 10X. I attended a 10X Growthcon event only because Daymond was a speaker. I realized it was a business community I could utilize to grow professionally, and that's precisely what I've done. Yes, it is an investment to be part of any business community, and 10X is not an inexpensive community in which to engage. But if I don't invest in myself, nobody will invest in me. And if someone already has a proven level of success, it's smart to learn from them and model that success.

Everything I have done has been with intention, and no job I've held has been without its rewards. I didn't have a father's guidance, but I had my mother's grit, my grandmother's strength, and a dream that refused to die. Along the way, I gained the wisdom of powerhouse mentors—especially Grant Cardone and Daymond John—who showed me how far resilience and vision can take you. Legacy isn't inherited; it's created.

# ABOUT GINGER KING

Known admiringly in the industry as *The Beauty Shark*, Ginger is an award-winning cosmetic chemist, entrepreneur, and speaker. She was born in Taiwan and raised by her mother and grandmother after her father died when she was an infant. Realizing the unlimited possibilities for her brilliant daughter in the United States, Ginger's mother brought her to America as a teenager. They arrived with little more than determination and a dream.

Ginger always dreamed of a career in cosmetics, and she began creating perfumes and other products in her dorm room as a chemistry student. Once she graduated with a B.S. in chemistry and a minor in business, she could only find a job in the food business, analyzing pineapples at Dole Foods. Knowing she wanted to be an entrepreneur in the cosmetic business, she soon earned an MBA as well as an M.S. in Chemistry. Within a few years, she was formulating multimillion-dollar beauty products, proving that every setback can become a stepping stone.

Her journey to entrepreneurship embodies resilience, vision, and bold reinvention. Today, she is the founder of **Grace Kingdom Beauty**, a consulting firm creating shelf-ready brands from concept to launch, and FanLoveBeauty, a clean vegan cosmetic line inspired by her mentor Daymond John of Shark Tank.

Crowned "The Queen of Cosmetic Chemistry" by *Elle* magazine, Ginger has been quoted in over 40 publications, featured on *Forbes, Inc.*, and *Success Magazine*, and named one of *Success Magazine's Top 50 Women of Influence*. She is also a certified **10X Business Coach** trained by Grant Cardone—who calls her proof of what's possible when you live the 10X Rule.

From underdog to industry icon, Ginger's life proves that no matter where you start, you can create beauty, business, and a legacy that lasts.

Ginger lives in New Jersey with her husband, Ronald, son, Martin, and mother, Ava.

 thebeautysharkginger

 gingerking

# What Are You Actually *Doing*?

### JOHNNY WIMBREY, Ph.D.

There's a big difference between being busy and being productive. Since I turned my life around about thirty years ago, I've focused on being as productive and successful as I can possibly be. I had already squandered the first two decades of my existence, and there was no extra time to waste—I intuitively knew my time was valuable and limited. I had extra incentive: I was in love, and my future wife and in-laws had great expectations for me, almost as big as I had for myself.

As I started gathering the skills and tools I needed to walk my new path, I did it without guidance or help. My new goals were all mine, simplistic and money-centric, and they centered around making a life that was worthy of Crystal, the woman I loved from the moment we met. She had faith in me, and I knew I couldn't let her down.

Two of my best assets were my innate sales skills and charisma, both unpolished but functional. My ethics came from watching my father, a trashman, as he called himself, work hard and do his best to be a single dad. I knew right from wrong, but what I knew was still black and white. My other assets were my good instincts: I have a burning desire to be around people who are successful so I can learn from them, and I never want to stop learning. Add in my awareness of the value of time, and I had the raw materials I needed to become spectacularly successful myself. Last but not least, I had faith in myself and in God.

The debit side of the balance sheet includes my ferocious temper and the unfortunate fact some of my friends in my crime-ridden neighborhood were in gangs. I had a teenage felony arrest and not much education. I didn't yet have any real mentors, though my future in-laws and a minister had hopes for me and I wanted their approval. There were no giants offering me shoulders to climb on to help me add to the bottom line. Not yet, anyway. The giants showed up in a couple of years and changed my life exponentially.

But at that moment, I was vulnerable. I had very little guidance, I yearned for success almost too much, and I was damn lucky I didn't get sucked into some crooked get-rich-quick scheme.

My college experience was at a fine arts school with an acting program. When I graduated, I knew I needed a job with flexible hours for auditions. Sales seemed to be a natural choice since I could control my own schedule. I'd worked as a telemarketer for two years while I was going through school, and that was a great start to a career as a sales executive. My acting experience gave me a patina of confidence, though I had always been uncomfortable speaking to people on a one-on-one basis. I knew I had quite a bit to learn, and I couldn't wait to get started making money.

The state of Texas offered a 90-day temporary insurance license; I obtained one easily and went to work for a large, well-respected national company while I studied for the state licensing exam. I wasted no time diving in and immersing myself in whatever I could learn about the business, and I was methodical and organized with my studying. What was key, though, was making calls, as many as I could make, and improving them, call by call, giving myself immediate feedback as I evaluated what worked and what didn't. I focused on the effective calls as I learned what my customers needed, what they wanted, and how I could help them. Working day after day, I refined my sales call to be better—a more *productive* call.

Before my three-month temporary license expired, I was already one of the top 50 salespeople in the entire company, selling more insurance than thousands of their most experienced agents. I was determined to pass the test and become the company's top-producing insurance agent. I was sure this was my path to success.

The licensing exam took three attempts, but I finally passed, took a deep breath of relief, and mailed in my application and test results. I had just turned 21 and I was sure I was on the cusp of becoming the successful, upstanding young professional I aspired to be.

Only a week later, my plan was in tatters. The Texas Department of Insurance rejected me because of my felony arrest the previous year, a permanent blot on my otherwise clean record. The original charge had been downgraded to a misdemeanor, which is why I was sure I could pass the background check, but the arrest had undeniably been a felony charge.

I was as close to panic as I had ever been. How could I appeal? I couldn't refute the reality of the charge and do a "deny, deny, deny" routine—it truly happened.

Then I made one of my first excellent adult decisions. I decided I had to own my mistake and see what I could do to get things fixed. I didn't throw myself a pity party, stick my head in the sand, give up, or get angry. Instead, I felt my resolve take shape. I wasn't *about* to give up, and it marked a key moment in my young, untested life.

I took a deep breath and called the clerk at the Tarrant County courthouse; that's where my arrest had been downgraded by The Honorable Wayne Salvant to Class C misdemeanor. I was shocked when the clerk said he and the judge remembered me. I asked, humbly, "Would you both be willing to write a letter on my behalf simply stating anything that would give me another chance with the state department of insurance?"

Both Judge Salvant and the county clerk agreed they would. In just a week, I received an envelope in the mail that looked exactly like the license rejection letter. Before I opened it, I prayed, then I told myself I deserved whatever was sent to me. If it was another rejection, I'd accept it as my due.

The envelope contained only my state license—*Johnny Dewayne Wimbrey, Health & Life Insurance Agent, Texas Department of Insurance.*

Learning the difference between being truly productive and just being busy is perhaps the most important distinction you can make if you want to become a top-producing modern giant yourself.

Be focused. Focus on what you accomplish versus how much you're doing. Results are not the same as activities.

First, of course, you must be able to analyze what you are actually doing.

It's all too easy to trick yourself, especially if you're not actively procrastinating or goofing off. Don't let the smoke and mirrors you've created fool the very person who needs to know the truth.

So, you did your training, you planned your actions, you know what you're supposed to be doing. You're busy. You're not wasting your time, you say, and let's even agree that it's a fair analysis and you're telling the truth. You're doing what you're supposed to do.

But ask yourself, is what you're doing **effective**? Are you producing or are you spinning your wheels, blowing smoke?

- Did your training teach you all you need to know?
- Is your planning well-targeted?
- Are your emails well-written?
- Are your calls generating results?
- Are your posts getting responses?
- Are you reaching your goals?
- Most importantly, are you *objectively evaluating your results?*

If that isn't happening, you might as well stay in bed.

In addition to learning how to focus, *you need to value your time.* This is hard for many people. They usually value other people's time and try not to waste it, but their own time stretches out in front of them, unlimited and unrestricted, begging to be wasted. Valuing and managing your time is something you must master before you move to the next level of productivity.

Begin by focusing on the accomplishment, not the activity. Don't be fooled by your good intentions and the many hours you spent working. Don't be waylaid by the lists you've made. These are all things you *did*—activities—not the positive results of your actions.

It's all too easy to become too busy to be productive. An analogy I often use is that being too busy is just like getting on an airplane headed in the wrong direction. A commercial jet is an awesome piece of equipment, costing many millions of dollars, staffed with trained experts in flight and safety, owned by a multi-billion-dollar company, and requiring coordination and planning by an army of support crew and air traffic controllers. But when you get on an airplane that's headed to the wrong city, it won't get you where you want to go, no matter how fast it flies or how good the champagne is in first class.

> Focus on what you accomplish versus how much you're doing

My years of being in sales and sales management convinced me that no matter how busy someone is, that does not equate to their being productive or successful. I've watched so many people fail because they are too busy to be productive.

Sales "blitzes" are prime examples of misguided energy. The sales manager whips the sales force into a frenzy, going full-bore, doing nothing but selling, for the full stretch of the blitz. But you're not in a World War II panzer tank, running over the opposing army, blindly crushing the opposition. These are your clients that you're running over! You need to make sure the flurry of activity doesn't waste your time and their goodwill.

Every contact you make with a client not only uses your limited time, but it has lasting consequences. Bad calls stick in your clients' memory, even if you forget them because of the frenzy you were in. An ill-conceived and poorly targeted call is more than just a waste of your time—it's a waste of the client's time too, and it leaves a bad taste behind, tainting their opinion of you.

Your careful thought and emotional connection must go into every contact you make. Each contact should be targeted and be part of your strategy. Each contact deserves your best efforts.

I recommend that you look at your well-filled calendar and evaluate the work you've planned for the next month. Are those tasks all productive, helping you reach your goals?

If the answer is no, start learning to be ruthless while you protect your time. Take those calls, events, and time wasters off your calendar. If you're afraid to cancel them altogether, at least delay them a week or two until you've had more time to analyze how you're spending your time.

Whenever you're spending your time doing things that don't help you reach your goal, you're moving away from that goal, just as though you'd been on the wrong airplane.

Now let's look at the flip side of how you've been prioritizing your schedule. Have you been putting off meetings or calls because you've been too busy? If these meetings and calls are in line with your true goals, this is the time to slot them into the newly created gaps in your schedule.

Also remember the unscheduled preparation time for each meeting or call is important because you want to do quality work. This time only counts, though, if your actions lead to you being productive.

We all know those people who should be top producers but haven't reached that elite level. You've met dozens of them, and I've met thousands. They're talented, organized, and focused. They even use their time fairly productively, but they never make it to the top. We'll continue to use salespeople as examples here, but this applies to any business person who misses becoming a top producer, in any field, at any level.

From the time I was in my 20s and still working in insurance, I trained sales organizations. Though I was a good manager, I could never get the whole team to reach elite levels of production. One group of salespeople always lagged and it was the same group every week. I analyzed the sales force, trying to find the variable, something I could adjust, the "X" factor.

As I looked for discrepancies that could explain the difference in production, at first I was stymied. Every sales team member was in the same office because 25 years ago, there was no such thing as working remotely. Each salesperson had the same management, the same administrative support, the same sales and time management tools, and the same training. They had equal access to the same products, all sold them at the same prices, and they shared the same quality leads. Each of them even spent the same amount of time following up with the leads. They were all chosen from the same pool of candidates and theoretically had equivalent intelligence and education.

After studying the patterns, I realized their results were a result of only one variable: *how they responded to the cards they were dealt.* I call this the *Me Factor.*

As an upper-level manager, I participated in the Monday morning sales meeting, a lively hour or more, where we'd rehash the previous week and discuss everyone's sales figures. My top producers always had one thing in common: Every week they had fantastic attitudes. They'd tell stories about how well the week went for them and share tips and stories on what worked especially well.

The lesser-producing salespeople had excuses, complaints, and problems. Without exception, they said they weren't to blame. I couldn't avoid the obvious conclusion: Their *attitude* was the "X factor" I was trying to identify. Nothing else was different.

The people at the bottom of everything (or anything!) are always the best at one single thing: They point the blame at someone or something else, *and it is never, ever their fault.*

During my career I've met tens of thousands of people from every walk of life. I listen to their heartbreaking stories, tragedies I expected should suppress their spirits, if not flat-out break their hearts. Instead, they show up full of enthusiasm, determined to sit on our shoulders, to learn, to look further down the path, and become more productive. Invariably, they have a fantastic attitude and keep it, no matter what's thrown their way. They don't wallow in depression and self-pity. They don't make excuses.

If you are reading this book, neither do you. You are never reliant on excuses. You're looking to improve your circumstances, your family's future. Your career. Your life. Eventually, your legacy. You fight to improve, to better yourself in every way that matters.

Years before I was a sales manager and gave the "Me Factor" a name, I switched my own attitude 180 degrees. The pivotal moment was when my best friend died in a gang shooting. For the first time in my young life, I knew I'd die too if I kept my vengeful attitude. I knew my dead friend would not benefit from any terrible thing I did in his name, and I realized I was probably headed to the same morgue. I decided on the spot to change my attitude, turn my gun in, and *not* go for blood as was expected of me. My future was not preordained, and I chose to change directions with my life. This was just before Crystal became part of this new life. Soon, she helped me find the right path and stay on it.

My decision and my new attitude led to a rich, rewarding life far beyond any of my adolescent dreams. I have spent more than 30 years encouraging others to follow my path and find true mental, spiritual, and physical wealth. No part of my life would have been possible if I hadn't changed my attitude when I was a teenager.

Siblings, though raised the same way by the same parents, can be on very different paths, with very different attitudes. From the paths we chose, we three Wimbrey boys could not be more different.

My brother Larry was in prison for most of his adult life. I was on that path, too, until I had the epiphany after my friend's death. Larry's sentences have all

> " It's all too easy to become too busy to be productive "

been served, and he's out of the prison system, making a new life now, thank God. He's a beloved and active part of my life and family.

Our brother Willie went on a diametrically opposed path, joining the ministry at the same time he left for college. He dedicated himself to becoming an educator, first a teacher and then junior high principal by the time he was 30.

I love to teach as much as Willie does, but in a very different way. My approach is to first learn and then I coach, mentor, and share my knowledge. If you want to learn, I want to bring you to success and I love every minute of the process. I can't imagine doing Willie's other job, though. My faith is deep, but I could never be a pastor.

We three brothers shared our upbringing and genes, and we are so very different. I say we are affected by the *Me Factor*. It's a matter of attitude, and attitude is a choice you make.

I'm not going to insult your intelligence by giving you a primer on how to set goals. I'm going to give you a graduate-level seminar on goals, instead. You already know you need to set goals if you ever hope to be a top-level producer. If you haven't yet realized this, you're not serious, so don't waste your time reading the next section of the book.

Before I wrote this chapter, I reviewed several other books I've written on success and rising to the top. *Setting goals* is one of the constants in my advice (and in my mentoring and coaching, and in the many talks I give). If you look up "goals" in one of my books' indexes, you'll find I've sprinkled them throughout the chapters, in different applications, in different levels of complexity. Goals in all their forms are listed more than any other aspect of success, and they're the core ingredients in your success, a key aspect of the recipe.

When you set a goal, you know what the prize is. But setting the goal is a meaningless exercise unless you know how you're getting to that point and intend to truly grab that brass ring. (By now we're assuming you're productive and have a positive attitude, the necessary prerequisites for reaching your goals. I did say this was a graduate-level course!)

The best visual representation I use for setting goals is a ladder. The goal is at the far end, at the top, and the rungs of the ladder are the necessary steps you use to get to that point. A ladder without steps is just a couple of useless poles, right?

During my first year in the insurance business, I made $54,000. The math is simple—I was earning just over $1,000 each week. After one year, I was experienced enough to know how to calculate what I needed to do to earn that much at a *minimum*. I broke down the math and wrote how many appointments to book, when I needed to do them, and how many sales I had to close.

Equally important, I also plotted points of no return. I was not going to slide down the ladder, reversing my upward arc. It was an inviolable threshold. I was not going to slide. Never again would I settle for less than my current level.

Each rung, in effect, became the bottom rung on my revised ladder. These points of no return kept me on my upward arc and at the same time, they kept me grounded. The goals seemed more attainable as I worked toward them, one step at a time. They weren't abstract in the least and they didn't look out of reach. I was already standing on the rungs, and that gave me confidence.

Some years, my goal increases were smaller than others, but I never slid down past any point of no return. As each goal increased my income, it was manageable. For instance, when my goal was $100,000 per year, double my original income, I knew I needed a certain number of meetings to make my $2,000-per-week income goal. I kept track of where I was, rung by rung. The process was familiar, manageable, and I had confidence in being able to reach the various steps on my ladder.

To aid my productivity, I added a variety of factors to my ladder in addition to the numbers. I knew, for instance, that I needed to book my week's appointments by early afternoon on Monday, so I set a goal of making 50 calls before 1 p.m. on Monday, setting up the 12 to 15 appointments I needed to make my goal for the week. Monday mornings after the sales meeting were always reserved for appointment-setting phone calls, and that time was inviolable.

We're not done with your goals yet. You'll need to master many aspects of building and reaching your goals before you can reach the pinnacle for which you yearn. I cover them in many of my other books, especially in *Building a Millionaire Mindset*, but I'll include one more in this chapter: *You need to set accountability check-ins.*

That means you can't hold yourself accountable all by yourself. You need help—in other words, an accountability partner. It might seem awkward to share your vision and goals with another person, but how else can they hold you accountable?

Share your goal with a good friend, a coach, or your mentor, and ask them to help you track your progress up your ladder. You need to choose someone who will ask you tough questions, who cares about you and your success, and who truly wants you to win. You both will keep track of the specific benchmarks you reach on your journey. I use the word specific carefully, because I learned that the hard way.

When I was writing my first book, *From the Hood to Doing Good*, I knew I couldn't keep my writing project secret. It was the first time I was writing anything major, and I needed a lot of help to keep myself on my schedule with something so new and different.

I chose my friend Christopher, a fellow student in our church leadership program. We were friends and shared many of the same goals. When I told him about my book project, I immediately knew he liked the idea and cared about the book, and he clearly wanted me to finish it. I asked him to help keep me accountable.

The first few months, he asked me how I was doing with the book at least twice a week, every time he saw me. Though I appreciated that he followed up with me so closely, I didn't realize I was actively undermining our accountability project when I just answered, "Fine," which was technically true. I may have made notes, done some planning, or written a couple of paragraphs in the few days between check-ins. I sure did a lot of thinking about the book, but very little writing. I honestly wasn't making much progress. As the months went by, I realized my attempt at accountability wasn't working.

The next time Christopher asked about my progress, I told him to specifically ask me how many pages I'd written to date. I knew that would keep me on my toes, because I absolutely had to give him higher numbers every time he asked. We were both surprised when it took me only one more month and nine accountability check-ins to finish my book.

As I refined my accountability partner concept, I also began to draw ground rules for the type of person I chose to be my partner. I was lucky with Christopher because he truly cared and wanted to hold me accountable. Someone who didn't have genuine interest in me should never be privy to my goals and visions.

Don't allow negativity into your innermost space, ever. You need support, care, and honest belief in your project, not skepticism. I could write a book about the dangers of letting negativity affect you. Oh wait, I believe I've done that already.

As my coaching and mentoring practice grew, I added a new twist: For every person you ask to help you as your accountability partner, offer to do the same for someone else. I think accountability should be a two-way street, and it can enrich your life to help others in such an important and supportive way.

Of course, you can also find an app or tracking system that will help keep you accountable. They're plentiful, and artificial intelligence (AI) is going to flood the market with glamorous new options. They may be efficient, but AI can't offer the extra element that people bring to relationships. When you bring in someone to hold you accountable, someone who cares for you, you don't want to let them down. It's a lot easier to blow off an AI partner than someone who deeply believes in you and your project.

> " You need to set accountability check-ins. "

I've set and met goals since I was 18 years old and turned my life around, and I know this has been the key to my success. I was shocked to learn that **80 percent** of people don't set any goals at all, not even New Year's resolutions. Americans are more likely to do the New Year's ritual, but those are mostly related to looking or feeling better.

There are many conflicting statistics, depending on which scientific study you read. But these numbers seem to be reliable:

- One-third of all people who set goals never track their progress at all.
- Only 8 percent of goals are ever met.
- 72 percent of goal-setters meet their goals when they write them down, make a plan, and give an accountability partner a weekly progress report.
- Setting challenging but achievable goals improves performance by 90 percent.
- The more specific you are when you set a goal, the more motivated you become, and the more likely you are to achieve them.

This means you will become a rare and accomplished person when you set a goal to accomplish something productive and to do better than you've done in the past. You'll have every advantage over the 80 percent of people who are content with their lives and never set goals.

Being an elite-level producer has been my life for thirty years; it's such a part of me that I can't imagine settling for mediocrity. I clearly remember the triggers and epiphanies I had when I began to excel at business at the end of my teenage years and early twenties, and I've shared some of them with you in this chapter.

A few years ago, I was in the middle of writing another book when my father died, and I remembered something he said to me that became the original trigger for my success, even if it took almost a decade to click into place.

My dad wasn't successful by most financial or career-defining metrics. He was a sanitation worker, a hard-working, hard-talking guy who could be a bit scary sometimes, but he raised my brothers and me by himself and did the best he could. When I'd lived with my mother, I'd been a poor student, even failing a grade, but from the moment I began living with Daddy, I had almost all A's and was near the top in my class. He had high expectations of what I should accomplish.

When I was 12, I brought home my first C since I'd moved in with him. It stood out like a glaring neon letter on my report card, and I wasn't happy to walk home with it in my hand.

Daddy scanned my grades. He didn't look up at me when he saw my C, and he didn't yell. He said something ultimately more cutting and memorable: ***Anybody can be average.***

Well, I'm not, and I'll bet you aren't either. So don't settle for anything less than life-changing when you set your goals.

# ABOUT JOHNNY WIMBREY

With one of the most stunning rags-to-riches stories of the century, Johnny has overcome his earliest memories of being hungry in a homeless shelter and his teenage felony arrest to become a multimillionaire entrepreneur, a sought-after coach, a world-renowned speaker, motivator, and best-selling author.

Johnny's best-sellers include ***Building a Millionaire Mindset***, a guide to successful entrepreneurship, and ***From the Hood to Doing Good***, which he wrote before he was thirty years old, already a millionaire and philanthropist, plus ***Multiple Streams of Inspiration***, ***The Power of Mental Wealth***, and, of course, ***Stand on the Shoulders of Multi-Million-Dollar Producing Giants*** in his new bestselling hardcover series.

His Mpower Empire's international clients include world-famous athletes, politicians, and elite leaders. Wimbrey Training Systems publishes the majority of his books and many of his co-authors' titles.

Most of the top names in personal development have asked Johnny to be on their stages, including the legendary speakers Les Brown, Zig Ziglar, and Jim Rohn. During his appearances around the globe, he has mentored and coached hundreds of thousands of elite leaders, multi-million-dollar entrepreneurs, and top producers.

He grew up as a biracial child from a broken family in one of the most dangerous and gang-ridden neighborhoods in Texas. A friend's death from a gang shooting gave him his first wake-up call, and then his life changed directions completely when he fell in love with Crystal, who had expectations for their future. He focused on his character and building a life for his family.

Johnny and Crystal, along with their daughters, Hannah and Psalms, and son, Honor, live in North Central, Texas.

 Wimbrey.com

 JohnnyWimbrey

 @wimbrey

# Can You Retire in Ten Years?

MEESHIE LEE

I was at a workshop when a new acquaintance asked me out of the blue, "Can you retire in ten years?" This simple six-word question changed my life. Actually, it's changed many hundreds of lives, because at that moment I had an epiphany and changed the direction of my life 180 degrees.

Now I'm known widely on social media under my brand, @ MeeshieMovesMoney. Yes, I'm an influencer, but I'm also a financial literacy educator and a financial services professional.

My brand is more than a brand to me. It's a crusade—to reach as many families as possible and teach them financial literacy. I teach people where to move their money, legally, and with far-reaching effect.

I work with families, small business owners, and anyone who is new to the concept of financial education. Not only do I teach them basic financial literacy, I teach them how to build wealth with intention and protect their legacies.

The company I partner with is a leadership development company that so happens to be in the financial services industry. We teach mindset. We teach strategy. We teach the things business schools leave out: How to lead with purpose and build something that lasts.

What I teach is exactly what I wish my family had access to years ago, before the real estate crash of 2008 took our investments and my parents' livelihood. I teach a way to end the outdated mindset that talking about money is wrong, or that it's greedy to want to have financial success, or that financial security and freedom is out of reach for most of us.

I most certainly didn't grow up fixated on financial success. My brother and I never talked about money with my parents, though we could see how it affected them. My dad is an ABC, an American-born-Chinese from New Jersey. Mom came to the U.S. for college; she left her life of privilege in South Korea for the chance of an exceptional education and unlimited potential in America. She soon discovered life in America didn't match the highlight reel she'd seen from Korea.

My parents became commercial real estate brokers, and had a nice house, drove nice cars, and projected success. It was mostly a facade. They were struggling to pay bills each month. I never really understood how hard it must have been for Mom to feel her life was sliding downhill. But now I get it. I see that same sense of defeat that shows up in so many people I work with, whether they say it out loud or not.

We're told to get a degree, work more than 40 years, and retire at 65. But how does that make sense? Even those who faithfully put percentages of their paychecks into their employer-supplied 401(k) accounts, IRAs, or Roth accounts have no idea what it means that their funds are invested in the stock market. Millions found out, though, when the market crashed.

I know people in their 60s, 70s, and 80s who saw $100,000 vanish from their 401(k)s. The younger ones faced not being able to retire, and some of the older ones had to start bagging groceries to pay their bills. Some members of my own family went through this, too. It's heartbreaking. How does it make sense? Do I want to live my life like that? Do I want my life to look like that? Absolutely not.

During my sophomore year in college, I was completely unprepared for what was truly happening in my family's financial reality. I was home for the weekend; I heard moaning coming from my brother's room, but he wasn't home. It sounded like someone in terrible pain. I didn't think to call for either of my parents. I just tiptoed to the door, which was slightly ajar. I peeked in and saw my mother, kneeling on the floor, crying, begging out loud for God to please help her and my dad out of the financial mess they were in. It was 2008. The real estate market had just crashed and banks were teetering. Their commercial brokerage company was flattened. To add another big blow, their dry-cleaning business failed; it was a big investment they'd made to fund their retirement.

I was aware of the luxuries Mom had been raised with and how she missed that lifestyle. Her parents had followed her to the U.S., and I knew what they'd left behind. While I knew she was unhappy with her financial status and stressed about paying bills, I had no clue just *how* miserable and frightened she was until that moment. She hadn't seen me, and I left her alone to mourn in privacy.

That night as I lay awake, all I could think about was how to get my family's finances in order. How could I help my parents and make sure I did not set myself up in the same pattern they had?

*I need to do something*, I thought. I didn't know what, or how, but at that moment I knew I'd break the cycle of financial struggle in my family. It took years longer than I expected, because I had no teacher or mentor. Since I found my way, I've done my best to be both to others.

Plenty of people have shared similar moments with me, witnessing their family members in such distress, experiencing it themselves, or both. Maybe, like my parents, they acted with the best of intentions and invested money into something that went wrong.

My brother and I were the only Asian kids in school, and we were relentlessly bullied. I wish I could say it didn't matter, but it did. Kids would mock my name, put their fingers in the corner of their eyes to make fun of mine, and treat me like I didn't belong. I think I buried a lot of it for a long time. It still stings now when I think of it. But I don't feel shame; instead, I feel fired up.

In eighth grade, one bully made it his mission to torment me. Day after day he'd come at me until I finally had enough, and I swung my lunchbox at him, right where it hurts. It wasn't the most diplomatic move, but it worked—he never tormented me again. That's when I realized I wasn't going to let people define me by my differences ever again.

Until that point, I'd just wanted to fit in. Now I began to love my uniqueness. I stopped trying to be like everyone else and started embracing the things that made me stand out.

Dance was already helping me find myself by that time, and it became my outlet. Dance taught me incredible discipline. I had started dancing almost every day a couple of years before—ballet, tap, modern dance—and I doubled down, preparing for competitions and pushing myself. Getting the rhythm and emotion just right was always a challenge, but when it clicked, it was magic. Dance taught me discipline. Though I played several instruments and took voice lessons, nothing mattered to me like dancing.

I loved it. I loved meeting new people from different schools. I loved being on stage. To be totally honest, I loved the attention! Even more than that, I loved the challenge.

I participated in National Young Miss Dance Ovations competition in high school, performing a theatrical dance inspired by Cinderella. My costume was a torn, dirty dress, and I poured my heart into that performance. I didn't know if I'd win, but I was all-in on the experience. And then I stood onstage, shocked, in front of my parents and teammates as my name was called at the awards banquet.

Winning was more than a trophy to me; it was validation. Winning reminded me that it matters when you do what you believe in and are passionate about, especially when it's hard. For the first time, I felt like

I could really be something. It proved to me that what others think of me doesn't matter, but what I believe about myself does. Even though I didn't pursue dance as a career, dancing gave me the confidence I still carry into every room.

Dancing taught me to show up even when it's hard, to keep going when I want to quit. Dancing also taught me how to own who I am, both on stage and off. It also taught me to celebrate wins.

> " Lead with purpose and build something that lasts "

Wins don't always come with trophies. Every time I help someone protect their future, that's a win. Every time someone joins my team and starts learning the mindset it takes to lead, that's a win. I celebrate them all, though I don't let myself get carried away. The next win won't happen by itself. I have to go back out there and earn it.

I've become so wired to take action that I sometimes have to remember we aren't all built this way. The fear of failure, in particular, is a common trap people fall into.

But me? I don't sweat the "what could go wrong" part of things. Something *always* goes wrong when you think about it. There will always be challenges, setbacks, and bullies out there. But rather than have excuses to avoid action, I know they're part of life and move right past them. I do have to remind myself not to confuse confidence with cockiness at times, though.

When I fail, I always try to make sure I fail forward, not back.

If you truly love something, do it. Don't be discouraged by others. Set some boundaries. You are living your life, not someone else. If your friends don't support you, give them another chance to see your point, and if they're still negative, find new friends. If your family doesn't support you, it's unfortunate, but you're an adult. They don't have the right to run your life.

When I went to college, information technology (IT) was the hot field, or so I was told. I graduated with a solid education in web design, communications, and marketing, and set out to join the workforce. To my shock, no one was hiring in my field. At least they weren't hiring me, and I couldn't even blame artificial intelligence back then.

My bills still needed to be paid, so I found an alternate path. I took a summer gig as a café attendant at a Lexus dealer, making coffee for the well-off crowd waiting for their cars to be serviced. Though it wasn't my dream job by any stretch, you'd never guess by how I waited on you. My customers weren't responsible for my happiness, but I realized I was responsible for their good experience at my counter. I showed up, smiled, and made them feel welcome.

My bosses noticed. They saw how I connected with people, how I treated every person as though they mattered. The company created a brand-new position for me, turning service guests into sales leads. It was my first lesson in what it means to create opportunity by simply being excellent at whatever you are doing.

After a while, I realized I didn't want a career in sales and I turned back to IT, first landing a job at a consumer help desk. I didn't love customer tech support. In fact, I really disliked much of the work involved. But I enjoyed enough of my work to stick with IT for years, working in different roles, finding my strengths, and eventually gravitating back toward marketing and events. I realize I was a strong young woman in a male-dominated world during most of my IT years. It was lonely, and I didn't have a mentor.

During that time, I also got married. I was young and still incompletely formed. I was confident about my professional path, but there was a void in my personal development. I didn't have confidence in myself and I felt I always needed approval from him. When my marriage failed after a couple of years, I wasn't happy, but I continue to appreciate it taught me about who I am, what to look for in a lasting relationship, and how to tap into the courage to admit something isn't working instead of allowing pride and stubbornness to make me stay. Looking back, I realized my marriage failed forward, in that sense.

And there I was, young, divorced, wondering what to do next, when COVID hit. I couldn't stand the thought of locking down in Boston. When my cousin and I heard Dallas, Texas, was open and functioning more normally, we booked a trip to check it out. I fell in love with Dallas and knew almost immediately that I wanted to move there.

Back in Boston, I searched for a job in Dallas. It didn't take long. It wasn't my dream job, though I can honestly say I probably wouldn't have recognized it then if it was, but it was a decent enough job to justify the move. I started looking for tenants for my Boston house, took my cat, Sebastian, and what I could fit in a couple of suitcases, hopped on a flight and never looked back. I didn't have a return ticket or a Plan B. I didn't have a place to live.

But I did have my faith, my spirit of adventure, and my confidence that I would figure it all out. Sebastian and I settled into an economical pet-friendly hotel until I found an apartment, and I went to work.

I knew it would take time to find the dream job that would lead me to my dream life. I also knew I wasn't going to wait for everything to be perfect before taking that leap. I was single, I didn't have kids, and I didn't owe anyone an explanation. My parents were supportive, and whatever reservations they may have had, they kept to themselves, offering only encouragement.

A lot of people wouldn't do what I did. They'd say, "I need to have a job lined up, an apartment, a full plan before I can make a move." And they never do it. One day they look up and wonder what happened to their dreams.

Not me.

If I could give advice to anyone feeling stuck, it would be this: Prepare what you can, but don't let preparation turn into paralysis. Find the one or two non-negotiables that matter most— the job, the city, or just the reason you're making the leap—and take the leap.

People talk about *paralysis by analysis* all the time. I get it. But for me it's the opposite. I believe in *momentum by movement.* Don't wait for the stars to align. Don't wait until you feel ready. Just go. You'll be amazed what falls into place when you put yourself in motion.

My first Texas job was definitely not something I wanted to keep. But I was still paying a mortgage back in Boston and soon I had an apartment and rent to pay in Dallas, stretching every dollar, trying to keep things afloat. To my relief, I soon had a tenant in my Boston house, but the hassles outweighed the benefits and I ended up selling the house after a couple of years.

For the first few months, when whispers of *Am I crazy??* entered my mind, I made sure to use that doubt as motivation instead of intimidation. Yes, it was a difficult time financially, but this was just temporary. I will never regret that leap despite the challenges. My move proved to me again how resilient I really am.

My temporary job led to a bartending gig, back to IT again, in the office, and then remote. I realized I'm not really built for the corporate world. I was on a hamster wheel, spinning from one job to the next, to the next. I was not moving forward in terms of finding my dream job, but I was getting stronger and sharper along the way. I always had this mindset: *Keep moving forward.* Even when you're bartending, even when you're broke, even when your tenants are late and your new job isn't great, *keep going.* Action creates opportunity.

When I had my epiphany about the corporate world, I began studying for my real estate license, remembering my early sales experience after college at the Lexus dealership. I never intended for real estate to be my life's work, but I thought it could supplement my IT work and perhaps lead me to the next stage.

The same day I joined a real estate brokerage as a newly licensed part-time Realtor, I was let go from my IT job. Fortunately, I have a deep faith and believe God speaks to us when we're willing to listen. Being let go from that job *had* to be a part of His plan for me. I prayed, and He answered, *I need you to focus on this.*

But what was *this*? I didn't fully understand it at the time. I was sure "this" wasn't real estate, and I knew that answer would reveal itself if I was patient and open to receiving it. It took two weeks.

A friend invited me out to attend a concert, and he introduced me to his friend, Ara. I had no clue Ara was actively scouting me. I thought we'd shared nothing more than a concert until he called and invited me to a workshop.

> When I fail, it's always forward.

I was glad to go. *Maybe this would lead to something important,* I thought. And it sure did. I showed up with an open mind, and what I experienced there blew me away.

Ara asked me, "Can you retire in ten years?" When I laughed and said "no," he asked seriously, "Are you open to talking about it?" His words rocked me, setting the stage for what I was about to learn. The people at the workshop were amazing. They were open-hearted, driven, purpose-filled. I felt the energy, the diversity, the love right away. This was exactly what I'd been praying for.

The room was vibrant with different colors, different cultures, different stories, with one united mission. I felt instantly connected. The energy was electric. The values aligned with mine. I was learning things that no one ever taught me in school or in business. I was finally being mentored and I learned that mentoring gets you where you need to be.

I was all in. The company and its community completely shifted the direction of my life.

God made it clear to me the next time I prayed: *I need you to break generational mindsets. I need you to break generational curses, because I created each of you to live abundantly and to maximize your potential.*

Yes, I work with a financial services brokerage, yet it's so much more than what you'd imagine that is. It's leadership development. It's growth. It's a ministry. And it's rooted in something real. In this community, we stand for something bigger: *Maximizing our personal thinking so we can help others unlock their God-given talents and abilities.* That mission speaks directly to me because this isn't just about money—it's about mindset. It's about legacy. It's about becoming the person you were created to be and helping others do the same.

This is exactly what I was born to do.

All the pieces fit together, and I could see how what I was about to do could change lives. In 2008, if my parents had one of the financial products that I now make available, they would have had fiscal liquidity, the ability to rescue their business, and another, better, more solid, non-risky source of retirement income. My mother would have been spared her grief and fear.

Even when the real estate market doesn't crash, investing in real estate can sometimes backfire. It's drummed into us: *The best investment you'll ever make is your home. Put all your money into the most house you can afford and wait it out.* The result? Too many people are house-poor. If they lose their jobs or have a medical emergency, they have no options.

Yes, in theory houses are repositories for money if you have equity in the property. But it's the opposite of a liquid asset. Try borrowing on the equity of your house if you've lost your job. Your banker will laugh at you. Ask the millions of people who were underwater in their mortgage how easy it is to get their money back.

I am all for home ownership, I'm not saying otherwise. I think owning a home is vastly satisfying, fiscally responsible most of the time, and aspirational. But too many people put all their financial eggs into the home ownership basket and have absolutely no recourse when they suddenly need money. I offer solutions.

I'm a wealth strategist. I can talk to you about deferring taxes, tax-advantaged growth, building wealth for generations to come, and whether you're risk-adverse. If I only had five minutes with you, I'd find out where you are in your life and make recommendations.

Life insurance isn't about death. It's about building wealth, freedom, and future security. It's about liquidity, or available cash, and it's about security and controlling risk. It's about living. It's one of the most powerful wealth-building tools most people overlook because of outdated thinking or cultural taboos.

Let's say you're between 20 and 30 years old, just getting started. You've got time on your side, but probably not much money. What you *do* have are the two things you can never get back once they're gone: your youth and health. At this moment, you're the youngest and healthiest you'll ever be, the ideal time to get a life insurance policy. It will cost a fraction of what it'll cost when you're older, or if your health goes downhill.

If you were to have cancer, heart attack, stroke, terminal illness, or a chronic illness, and survive, OR be critically injured, and you couldn't bathe or feed yourself (or do any two of the six common daily activities), then you can receive a lump sum from your death benefit tax-free. The money can be used as tax-free income, to pay medical bills, for household or caregiver help, or in any way you want.

Most people don't realize that you don't get workers' compensation if you get hurt outside of work, in a car accident or at home. You need to use whatever personal time your employer offers, and it's limited. Few people have much in the way of either long- or short-term disability pay. When your vacation and sick time run out, you better hope you have hefty savings. But what if you *don't* have savings, like the majority of Americans? Few people have family resources or friends who can afford to help them out.

Certain policies come with cash value where your premiums become your assets. In effect, you're building a nest egg. As you pay into your plan, your money grows through compound interest. It's uninterrupted growth, which means even when life throws a punch, your money keeps working for you. Down the line, you can borrow against it without paying a penalty or taxes, like you're charged when you dip into your 401(k). You can use it as down payment, an emergency, or even to buy yourself breathing room when you're strapped.

Now let's shift your timeline. Say I'm sitting across from you when you're in your 40s or 50s and not where you thought you'd be financially. Perhaps you've been raising a family and putting the kids through college. No savings, not much in a retirement plan, just the stress of making it paycheck to paycheck. I've had that conversation more times than I can count.

My first question is always *Do you have any coverage at all?* And if the answer is no, then we work with what you do have: your income, budget, and your willingness to start now. Even if it's just $40 or $50 a month, I could help you find a policy that fits with the understanding you can always scale up later. The important thing is that you don't waste more time.

And what about someone over 50 who's really starting over? Maybe you lost everything in a crisis; market crash, health scare, divorce. You feel like it's too late. But it's not.

There are still options. If you don't have a retirement account, we can set you up with a final expense policy so your family isn't burdened with funeral costs. If you *do* have an old 401(k) or any money just sitting in your bank that didn't perform well, we can roll it over into a safer vehicle like a fixed index annuity that doesn't lose money when the market tanks. Not all fixed index annuities are created equal. That same annuity can even generate guaranteed tax-deferred lifetime income. That means monthly checks, coming in like clockwork for the rest of your life.

In fact, I tell my younger clients about these options too. If you start building a cash value policy now, later in life you can roll those funds into an annuity and set up guaranteed income for the rest of your life. That's how you retire *on your terms.*

There are far more complicated and sophisticated products as well. Everything is customized to the client's needs and goals, whether they're real estate investors or a couple building their nest egg.

But the real issue? It's mindset. The cultural stigma that makes us afraid to talk about money or death. The belief that a 401(k) alone is enough, even though it's tied to an unpredictable stock market that could crash any time. There are risks, but you can only make decisions with the information you have. If nobody tells you about these options, how can you decide to use them?

> " But the
> real issue?
> It's mindset. "

That's why I do what I do.

I'm glad I can't go back and change the years after college. I had to go through what I went through to get here. The failed jobs. The failed marriage. All of it shaped me. God's timing is perfect.

And when I look at my team today, when I see how many people I've helped protect, how many leaders I'm developing, and what a strong leader I'm becoming, I'm reminded that every bit of what happened to me matters. Every mistake. Every pivot. Every bit of financial literacy I've absorbed and passed on to others.

This is about more than money. It's about freedom. It's about peace. It's about knowing that no matter what life throws at you, you're not starting from scratch. Instead, you're starting from strength. That's what I hope for you, too.

When you lead with your heart, put your mind to something, and stay rooted in faith, God will take you exactly where you're meant to be. That's been true in my own journey, and it's what I want to pass on to others.

I want my legacy to reflect my faith, resilience, and purpose. I want people to say, "Because of Meeshie, I believed in myself. Because of her, I built a better life."

While I'm not here to push faith on anyone else, it's the foundation of everything I do. I'm open about that. Faith is a big part of my story.

My vision is bigger than me. I will build leaders. I will produce at least ten millionaires. I will open offices in Boston and beyond. I'm not just building a business. I'm building a movement because I believe God created us for more. He didn't design us to play small or think safe. He gave us the ability to maximize our gifts not just for ourselves, but to influence and uplift others. That's what *legacy* really means to me: living fully, giving freely, and helping you do the same.

# ABOUT MEESHIE LEE

A former information technology (IT) professional and now a financial services expert and educator, Meeshie Lee brings her money-management knowledge to underserved communities. She is a strong leader, finding her calling in helping families avoid fiscal pitfalls, reach retirement and generational wealth goals, learn about tax-advantaged strategies, and enjoy the safety of financial liquidity.

Meeshie was in college when she learned first-hand what it meant to lose everything. Her parents, both commercial real estate brokers, were brought down by the 2008 financial crash. Years later, she used her memories of that painful time when she found her calling in financial literacy education. Both her knowledge and deep faith help people shift their mindset and create legacies of abundance. Even when she's creating content on social media under her well-known handle @Meeshiemovesmoney, she's advocating for economic security and positive change—one household at a time.

After she graduated from Bentley University with a degree in Graphic Design and Marketing, Meeshie spent more than a decade working in IT, some of those years in consumer tech support. She was a natural listener, and she learned to understand what people mean and fear most, not just what they say. When she moved to financial services, she was able to translate the unstated money fears people have, understand their outdated prejudices, and recognize the short-sighted habits that lead to fiscal mistakes and losses.

She believes people need to move out of their comfort zone, and Meeshie practices what she preaches. During the pandemic, she moved from Massachusetts, where she was born and raised, to start a new life in the Dallas/Fort Worth Metroplex, where she still resides with her cat, Sebastian.

Facebook: MeeshieMovesMoney

IG: @Meeshiemovesmoney

TikTok: @meeshiemovesmoney

# What Are You Here to Do?

## KATE STONE AND ZAC GORDON

As a couple, we're greater than the sum of our individual parts—we recognize we're more powerful when we work together. Having this edge is a necessity because we're taking on a gargantuan task: We're trying to change how people see education, to *crack the nut of education*. It's worth every bit of effort we put into our goal. We know breaking it open will change the lives of countless young people for the better.

Our goal sounds deceptively simple: It's for students at any level to succeed in their lives.

We want teenagers and young adults to discover what they're *meant* to do with their lives, not what they're *expected* to do. We don't want them to find out their true calling when they're thirty or fifty, but when they're still young enough to make the most of the opportunities that are there to help them start their adult lives. We want them to change the trajectory of their lives, starting as young as possible. We help them find what will enrich their lives, to go in the direction that they're meant to go.

We have both practiced what we preach, though we each took a long, roundabout way of finding what we were meant to do. We found our way eventually by doing what we loved, and by taking unconventional life paths—not just what we or others thought we should do. We discovered we both thrive on taking risks, and we learned what a rare quality that is.

We hope to make it easier for others to find their own way, with the guidance and support we wish we'd had along the way. So many students say they want to go into a certain field but have no idea what it involves. Part of our work with students is to have them deeply research what is required to reach those goals and allow them to realize for themselves if they have what it needs to pursue that field or profession. We have them do the same research when they're choosing colleges, which are often not what their name or reputation implies.

We have a unique coaching business, helping kids find their futures and their missions—the schools, the careers, the niches where they'll excel. We don't just take the best and the brightest high-school students and funnel them into elite colleges, though we've done our share of that. We help them find their *future*, one they'll love and where they'll thrive.

We try to start with students as young as possible and stick with them as long as possible. If we're lucky enough to be able to work with kids starting in middle school, we stick with them through high school, through college and internships, and when they graduate, we coach them until they find the job that's right for them.

The two of us work together, complementing each other's skills and knowledge: Again, we're more than the sum of our individual parts. Kate is the face and voice of the business, and Zac is the growth driver and key educator. He's taken our joint expertise and turned it into a curriculum other qualified coaches can deliver, expanding our reach exponentially.

We knew when we met that we were meant to teach together. Together, we teach kids to identify their values, dreams, desires, talents—their way of being totally and uniquely themselves.

Knowing what you truly are is success, boiled down to its core. Children can only do this by leveling themselves up, pursuing experiences that help them grow, and by figuring out which of their interests are the vehicles they need to help them be successful in life.

This is where we come into our students' lives.

While most parents honestly want their children to be happy, fathers and mothers can flounder without support. It's remarkably tough these days just to parent, to indulge in a rarely used verb, and that is why we involve the entire family in our coaching.

Our coaching system doesn't ignore what kids are already accomplishing in school, nor does it focus solely on helping them get better grades and get into top schools. If a coach does that, they're already failing their clients. Our system identifies interests and priorities and adds new emphases to how they spend their time.

We prioritize three pillars. We teach kids to:

1. **Identify** and solve problems in their communities so they can have a meaningful impact on the world around them.
2. **Build** stacks of evidence in their areas of focus that prove they are interested in what you say you are.
3. **Combine** the story, brand, and network:

*Find* and tell the story of who they are and why anyone should care.

*Discover* their personal mission and how to achieve it.

*Find* mentors and advisors, and build networks that support them and their pursuits.

Supporting the parents and the family is a natural extension of what we do with our kids. Their lives are mostly spent at school and at home, and everything we do is meant to enhance their full lives and not stop at the door when they leave home.

What parents don't understand is that their children are dying for someone to *see* them for what they are, give them guidance, and even sometimes directly tell them what to do. Yes, usually kids hate getting orders, especially from parents, but they need them sometimes. Many parents can't believe it, but as counterintuitive as it may seem, teenagers do need direction, and the more disengaged, lost, and apathetic they are, the more they need it.

When parents and their children come in at loose ends, not knowing how to reach some kind of successful result, we try to see if the parents themselves are demonstrating what they want in their kids. If the parents embody what they want their children to do, our next question is, were the kids shown what to do, ideally at an early age? How much practice have they had developing these skills? Have they practiced chores initiative or other skills 100 times? One thousand times? If not, why do the parents expect success?

Most parents are too busy to make the time to work with their children in this focused and repetitive way. This is why we exist. It truly does take a village.

Children will rise to the level of expectation that's being set for them, assuming they have the education, support, and practice to meet those standards. It's about the amount of commitment the parents put into it, and that's an exciting proposition for a child who wants to succeed and get out into the world without being limited. In most cases, there's no mechanism to help them reach that point. And it's damn unfortunate, because most kids don't want to be limited; they want to fly.

Kate knows this firsthand; she was desperate for direction when she was young. She didn't bloom until she was out of college and some incredible adult mentors gave her advice and encouraged her to explore.

As intimately involved as we are with our clients and their families, we don't share much personal information with them; we keep our boundaries in place at the same time as we immerse ourselves in a family's habits and goals. But our personal childhoods and twenties, as unusual as they were, set the stage for our success in adulthood and so we need to share some background with you.

Kate had a difficult childhood as part of an alcoholic family. Though she loved teaching and earned a B.S. in education from NYU, she wasn't sure of her future until she was awarded a post-graduate Princeton teaching fellowship in Bali and Thailand. Zac's childhood was much easier, growing up in a supportive family, believing he could do anything, and always thinking out of the box. After trying out several possible careers, he focused on education, teaching in high schools, colleges, and to hundreds of thousands of online students.

> " We're trying to change how people see education, trying to crack the nut of education. "

Kate's family suffered from addiction; her father's alcoholism finally tore the family apart. There was a lot of uncertainty in her life, and they moved almost every year when she was young. When they moved to New York City, her grandparents filled in during the week for her mother, an intensely driven medical malpractice litigator. Kate lived for the weekends when she was able to spend time with her mother, who made each errand and outing into an adventure. Her mother believed in her wholeheartedly and encouraged every one of Kate's dreams. Every child should be as lucky as Kate was in that aspect of her life. But it wasn't enough to give her direction or help her discover her strengths.

Kate hated school and drifted through the system without any guidance or vision of where she might land. The family ethos was "You need education to survive," but she was struggling. Her teachers said she was "creative," which is often "teacher-speak" for "not too intelligent."

She wasn't mediocre at all, though; she was uninspired and bored by the curriculum and how she was being taught. She was looking for some direction. In high school, she finally cracked the code for getting good grades and learned how to do the bare minimum needed to get into New York University (NYU). Kate imagined a college experience brimming with intellectual challenges, somehow finding inspiration, determining her direction, and becoming tremendously good at something she hadn't yet figured out or perhaps imagined.

Of course, NYU turned out to be just a tougher and more expensive version of high school, and nothing clicked. Kate made it through all four years and graduated with the grades necessary to qualify for a four-year teaching fellowship at Princeton University. She left for a second four-year commitment, teaching in Thailand and Bali, buzzing around on a bright green Kawasaki motorcycle, tutoring kids as part of her fellowship program.

Kate finally found her bearings when she was introduced to several remarkable people who became her mentors, and they saw promise in her when she didn't see it in herself. Jonathan became a father figure and mentor to her, something she'd searched for and needed for a long time. As they talked, Kate began to realize she loved storytelling and performance, and she developed a growing desire to act. Jonathan had worked with Sir Ridley Scott, the director-producer of 50 major films, and he'd also worked on many commercial campaigns, including Nike's. That became their personal joke, and often he'd say, "You know what Nike said, Kate, *just do it!*"

So, with Jonathan's guidance and support, Kate kickstarted her new career. Over two-and-a-half years, she honed and improved her acting skills. She found an acting teacher, and after acting in every possible venue available in Bali, she moved to Singapore, where she acted in NYU student films. With this experience under her belt, she next moved to Indonesia, where she had a good role in a feature film. Finally, she felt she was ready to move to Hollywood, where she had a successful ten-year stretch, acting in both commercials and television shows.

Perhaps the most important guidance Jonathan gave Kate was when he told her seriously, "Pay attention to this part of your life [teaching], because it's going to become more important as you get older." She followed his advice, and in Hollywood, she turned to tutoring between acting gigs rather than waitressing.

While still in Hollywood, she developed her own style of college prep tutoring, focusing on finding the student's true interests and talents and not just focusing on an application essay. Soon, using her storytelling abilities, she found a way to trigger the students' stories and inspire them to write a much more revealing and authentic essay.

In addition to finding more memorable mentors over the years, Kate also found support in Al-Anon, the organization for families and friends of alcoholics. Children of alcoholics grow up with an outsized sense of responsibility and a variety of repercussions, including post-traumatic stress from the disease that one or more parents may be afflicted with. Attending Al-Anon family groups gave her a new set of tools, helping her reeducate herself and find some incredible mentors. With the help of those mentors and others in Al-Anon, she learned to set boundaries and remind herself that she was not responsible for fixing everyone's mistakes and problems.

Kate's strengths include her ability to talk to anybody with ease and openness to find out what's important in their life, and her deep authenticity.

Zac took a more circuitous route to his current key role in Kate Stone Prep. He is an archetypal teacher, but you would never have known it when he was a student.

His earliest memory is from when he was three years old, and he asked, "Why are we here? What's the meaning of life?" He and his sister grew up thinking they could do anything, and he didn't realize until later in life what a big gift that was.

Their dad was an entrepreneur and dropped out of school to start his own business. Zac, like Kate and his dad, also found school unchallenging, monotonous, and boring, and he dealt with it more demonstrively than Kate did: He skipped school, often and with gusto. He would have told you he was looking for the juice of life, or perhaps the school of life, which to him was more real than formal education.

He decided to drop out and go find that juice while he was still in high school. That was the beginning of a cycle of dropping out then returning to finish both high school and college at the top of his class and with honors. (Ironically, he returned to teach at his old high school.) He always thought outside the box, but he realized early he needed mentors and sought them out, finding some amazing ones who guided him.

He earned a series of degrees and sampled a variety of careers as a young adult. Zac became a professional musician, an agriculture student, and then a farmer. He also found time to study Sanskrit, an ancient Indo-Aryan language.

Zac never stopped searching for the right mentor, someone to help him make sense of the world and find his calling. One of Zac's mentors, Lee Ching, told him, "You're not going to be here forever. You will need to go out and teach this to the world." That became Zach's next career turn, and he taught in high school and college, and to hundreds of thousands of professionals through online courses.

We both incorporate much from our travels and our mentors. Zac, in particular, absorbed a tremendous amount of information from his adventures around the world. We are taking the best of what we learned at the various stops in our journeys and applying it to our coaching, mentoring, and teaching.

We believe the purpose and direction you choose is dependent on the mentors in your life. We know absolutely that what you believe you can achieve depends on the pathway you were shown.

That's why we take a variety of children, not just the ones ready to write their college essay, help them find and explore the topic that sparks their interest and help them find their paths. It may seem unlikely, but in every case, they're fully engaged. They're stoked. They're ready to explore this interesting new direction. When we describe our process to adults, almost all of them react with astonishment and delight, with many saying, "God, I wish I'd had a mentor, someone helping me in that way when I was a teen and young adult. I would have found my calling so much quicker and easier."

> Most kids don't want to be limited; they want to fly.

Yes, we know. We would have, too. Our belief is that every child could use this help. Every parent, too, for that matter.

When a young teenager tells us they've chosen their field, they're usually not aware of what is truly involved. They have probably researched the education they'll need but may be unaware of the character and type of personality involved in certain jobs, and the networking that is a part of its success. Often they're influenced by parents or what they see in their surroundings, not their innate inner drive. A child who wants to be a rich, multi-million-dollar hedge fund owner, let's say (don't laugh—there are many of those in Greenwich, Connecticut, where we're headquartered) might soon realize they don't have the drive they need to pursue an intense, dog-eat-dog career.

We have many kids who plan careers in law or medicine. We arrange for them to talk to professionals and map out the 16-to-20-year journey they took to get where they are, and discuss the ups, downs, sacrifices, and rewards of those journeys. Often, the students end up shifting their goals. We've had future doctors become future humanitarians, and future engineers decide corporate leadership and sales would be a better fit. Smaller shifts are often made, too: our future pediatrician who changed her focus to cardiology, or a fledgling electrical engineer who realized aerospace engineering was much more intriguing to him.

The same thing happens when teenagers are fixated on attending a certain college. Often it's something they've been told about the school that sticks in their imagination, or a glamorous event, like a national championship, or the fact that a relative attended it and loved it. If their parents attended and they're a legacy student, the desire might be strong but not thought-out at all. Once they really research the college down to the program level, they'll often realize they loved the idea of the school, perhaps its name or game, but they realize it wouldn't be a good fit.

We think one of the dangers of our industry is equating what college a student gets into as a level of success. We argue that what a student is doing in a program, their success in learning independently, finding mentors, making more progress than they thought possible, are true measures of success, not just getting into a "top-ranked" school. Even at Harvard, they have a bottom 50 percent of each class that's not competing or learning the way they should be. *Every* top school has that same stagnant bottom 50 percent. That's not where our students should be. We want them to excel and enjoy the process.

With artificial intelligence being just the most recent factor in the job market, we are looking years ahead for our students' careers. We've recognized the shift in hiring is to a skills-first trend. It's even a *skill* to be successful now. I know, as an employer, that's what we're looking for in our employees.

One of our surprise students was Liam, the black sheep of his family, he and his parents thought and informed us. He had no idea what he wanted to be, but then he finally began to see he was in a great place to find out. He loved nature and as he explored it further, he realized environmental science was a strong option. We helped him identify possible career paths. To his delight, he found out he was technically proficient, and he built up skill sets to become even more so. He began actively building up his hard and soft skills to be more competitive, launching an environmental club at his school, and he truly became a leader.

Sometimes it's hard for kids to find meaningful impact projects. Liam found a void and went ahead and created a solution. He built a small but strong organization while still in high school, learned to interview people, identify good leaders for his group, built a network in the community, and began to create opportunities where they hadn't existed. He was well on his way to a successful adult career before he graduated from high school.

Zac works as a community builder, helping our students translate educational bits in the curriculum into skills they will use the rest of their lives. They learn how to galvanize and organize people. These are the most valuable skills a teenager can learn that they'll use and benefit from their entire lives, and they're often not taught these skills at all.

Where families have anecdotes, we have data. That not only sets us apart from other coaching organizations, it helps us educate the parents. We have an elite program, and it's exceptionally rigorous. Quite often parents think their child is at an elite level, but they're working with no context. This can sometimes have tragic results when their expectations are not backed by their children's capabilities. Not all children have the aptitude, portfolio, drive, or interest to compete at the highest levels. Some children are observers, helpers, or workers.

An important part of our program is to assess the personalities of our enrollees and see what they're naturally best at and find what types of roles and abilities they want to develop—and what they're able to develop. Sometimes they discover they *are* capable of elite performance, but it can take some strategic planning and hard work to get to that point.

Two years ago, two parents came to us and said their daughter, Anita, "is an artificial intelligence (AI) genius" because she'd gone to a summer AI program. That's admirable, but not necessarily enough to be proficient, much less a genius. We ran Anita through the gauntlet, had her start taking high-level deep math courses, rapidly upping her skills to the collegiate level, and she did well. That took care of the math issue, but we needed to make her a double threat, which is what we do as often as possible with our students.

Rather than have just one good interest, we want our students to develop two or three. A triple threat that overlaps is virtually impossible for any college to ignore.

With Anita, physics was the overlap. Her physics skills became so good we had to find her a physics mentor—one wasn't available for her even at the top private school she attended. We found her a college professor who was incredible.

Now Anita is doing advanced research. She has excellent technical skills and direction and a remarkable ability to assess programs. She's researching colleges to attend, and we have every confidence in her ability to find the one that's right for her. We know she's now at the level that wherever she goes, she'll be able to leverage her experience and make the most of it. She'll come out on top.

Teaching our kids how to research is one of our key strengths, and we believe it's one of our most important areas of focus.

Teaching them how to communicate is another. We want them to be able to research people, find the right person to reach out to, send emails that get attention, and then do follow-up. Teaching the skills of cold outreach is so important; it serves a person for their entire adult life. In Anita's case, one of the mentors she reached out to was featured in a national magazine as a leader in the AI revolution.

Then there was dynamic Beckett, a boy who came to us with an interest in marketing because he thought it was intriguing and exciting, but he had no idea what it took. In short order, we showed him how to find mentors, learn real marketing, take on a real business, and redo every one of its marketing assets and offers, find leads, convert leads, and most importantly, open up new opportunities.

Beckett drastically changed every aspect of that business, adding new opportunities that he researched and developed. He now knows more about marketing than a new graduate with a bachelor's degree in the subject.

In Kate's original coaching business, many of her clients were last-minute students who wanted to get into specific colleges. Chelsea came to her with a big goal—wanting to be admitted to Williams College. She wasn't at the top of her class, unfortunately, so her task was to build out an inviting application, one in which her essays and stories would sing. Her original essay about living overseas during her middle childhood had emotion, but no real story. Kate finally discovered Chelsea's passion: mountain climbing with her brothers, which she believed could bring Chelsea into a time and place. Kate asked Chelsea to outline a story, write about the mountains, what it's like to climb cliffs, explain some of the technicalities, fill it with little vignettes, and talk about how time in the wilderness with her brothers influenced and shaped her values.

> We believe the purpose and direction you choose is dependent on the mentors in your life.

Chelsea ended up writing one of the most beautiful college entry essays Kate has ever read. It was poetic and proved that if we can connect the students with what really brings them joy, it translates on the page, even if they're not the best writers. Writing from what you love and know is always the best strategy for success.

It's unfortunate that when parents try to influence their child's writing, usually from a place of fear or insecurity, they end up diluting the voice and railroading the child. As editors, we are trying to pull the child's voice out so it sounds like it belongs to an authentic 17-year-old, not someone doing their master's thesis. When you read it, you should know who the writer truly is, and it should never be the parent.

Our business model, as unusual as it is, and as expensive as the coaching process can be, includes a lot of pro bono work. We work with hundreds of families for free through our weekly seminars.

Our business is in a rapid growth model, and we are hiring new coaches on a constant basis. We are excited to grow the team to serve thousands of families.

While our current coaching business is mainly done on-site, not via the internet, our long-term goals include developing and rolling out a homeschooling course. It will fit seamlessly into the coaching of the parents and students both—that is such an integral part of the business we have now. As we build our own family, we will start developing curriculum and support for younger kids as well. And at the other end of the spectrum, more and more of our families want our help launching their kids successfully into their careers, not just into college, because these days, it is not enough to send children into their futures with a college degree alone.

Our students are our family, and helping them find lives that enrich them, that they enjoy and thrive in, is the reward we are given at the end of the process. We have found our niche, and while it's growing and evolving to something we had not imagined when we began, it really hasn't changed at all.

Our legacy will be the lives that our students live, the success they have in life, and most of all, what they add to the world.

# ABOUT KATE STONE AND ZAC GORDON

Partners in life and in cutting-edge leadership in the educational and college prep field, Kate Stone and Zac Gordon are redefining education in the 21st century. Both teenagers and younger children benefit from the coaching and mentoring their firm, Kate Stone Prep, provides to their entire families. Mainly, Kate Stone Prep helps children find and define their paths to extraordinary lives.

Kate strengthened and enhanced her teaching skills through an educational fellowship at Princeton University, and for four years, she taught and tutored in Thailand and Bali. Her natural love of storytelling led her to a successful acting career in Hollywood and abroad for the next ten years. During that time, she continued to use her strong teaching and mentoring skills to coach teenagers through the college application process into top schools. Seeing flaws in the current college prep process, Kate realized the need for longer and deeper mentoring of students.

When Zac also realized his affinity for education, he taught in high school, at the college level, and to thousands of students through online courses.

Kate Stone Prep, their rapidly growing coaching business, not only helps students find and get into the college that is right for them, but also supplies mentorship from an early age, ideally middle school, helping students find their way and fully understand the path they're on. Their students learn how to find mentors, do effective research, and make cold calls. Kate and Zac's company follows their students through college, adding coaching to help launch their post-college careers.

Kate is the face of their firm, and Zac is the educational core, creating curriculum for their coaches to use as they expand to reach thousands of students. Their plans include support for even younger children as they begin their family, and homeschooling curricula.

Kate and Zac live and work in Greenwich, Connecticut.

 katestoneprep.com

 Kate Stone College Coaching

 @katestoneprep

 @katestoneprep

# Nuture Your Hope

RYAN HILL

Everyone has a different concept of *hope* and how and where it fits into their lives. I wasn't able to access my own supply of hope until I finally shed the fear of failure that had always polluted and limited my life. Once I was free of my burden, I built a new business model based on the concept of instilling hope in my employees and business partners.

Though I own a roofing company, Trusted Roofing, you could say I deal in hope for a living. These days, I feel so strongly about the benefits and functions of hope that I created an acronym to reflect the culture in my company:

**H**elping

**O**thers

**P**ursue

**E**xcellence

Recently, my spirits were buoyed when I found some data compiling scientific studies of hope. I'd done an AI search, and after ChatGPT led me down 40 or 50 rabbit holes, I found this conclusion: "Scientific research robustly supports the power of hope as a transformative force in human life. It is associated with improved mental and physical health, greater resilience, higher achievement, and stronger social bonds. Importantly, hope is not an innate trait, but a skill that can be nurtured through intentional strategies and supportive environments."

All my life I've read about hope in the bible, where there are hundreds of different verses on the subject. I know in my heart that these verses are true, and when science backs up the bible, it's a beautiful thing.

My goal is to change the commonly accepted view of how a business should be run and how it should treat its employees. I don't have an MBA (and never plan to earn one) or a long history of owning and building businesses, but I am certain I'm right about a couple of key points:

- The company must value the team more than it values the customer. No, the customer doesn't always come first. Never forget your team is your greatest asset.
- People—not money—are the greatest business metric.
- Your company's business culture must nurture hope and the individuals who work there.

Anything else is short-sighted. You'll eventually lose your customers if your team doesn't feel valued. Of course, your bottom line matters, and we all agree you can't survive without a profit. But when your team begins to experience hope in their lives, potential is unlocked, and results begin to appear. *The profit will be there.*

When your focus is on your team and building hope in their lives rather than on profit, don't worry that you'll lose sight of yourself and your mission. Again, the profit will be there.

The culture in my company is very intentional. We've created an environment where everyone's helping everybody. We all accept that this is part of our company's structure. We all want to see *everybody* on our team succeed. I mean that seriously, and it bears repetition: Everybody on our team wants to see every other person succeed.

When we see others on our team succeeding, this gives the rest of us hope and encouragement to succeed as well.

So far we *have* succeeded. We started at zero when I founded my company from scratch. In just two-and-a-half years, we've billed more than $17 million in business.

Let me explain how I got to this point.

My family of five spent all our time together. I have two sisters, one older and one younger; we'd eat dinner together and clean up in a cooperative effort. Then, we played games with our parents—card games, board games, sophisticated stuff. And we all played seriously and competitively. We kids weren't locked in our own individual bedrooms, playing video games or watching television, except for sports, of course. The games my family played together during my childhood taught me many strategies that have helped me as an adult.

We shared other similar interests. We all sang, and my mother and younger sister played piano, while Dad coached all my sports. All of us kids were expected to volunteer wherever we were needed, at church or at school. I always knew I could count on my family. They were committed to me and expected me to show the same commitment to others. I had no choice in the matter, I was taught—it was my priority.

I eventually started going to geeky game stores to acquire more complicated games because nothing interests me more than strategy. Even when I was well into my twenties, I was still playing games with my friends while we watched the Kansas City Chiefs' football games. We were poker nerds, but we'd play every kind of challenging game that required some skill to win versus just random luck. This routine is no longer a big part of my life, but I'll always be up for games, and fortunately, it's contagious. My wife, Ashley, who swears she's not competitive, takes me on and becomes extremely competitive when we play cards together.

In the Midwest, playing sports and watching important games are both very big deals, and I love sports. I was active when I was younger, playing baseball, basketball, and golf, which I took up when I was eleven. Sports have the beneficial side effect of teaching discipline and networking skills, and the sports I played benefited me through those lessons. I enjoyed the common bond I shared with my teammates.

In addition, I was pretty good at what I attempted. At one point, I had a single-digit golf handicap, though now I struggle to break 90 because I don't get to play as much as I'd like. I'm glad I learned at least one game I can play forever, and I look forward to playing with my three children as they grow up a bit more. When my son goes to golf camp; he's learning to love the game and absorb its discipline, sportsmanship, and etiquette.

My other big love is music. I started learning to play the saxophone in fifth grade, and once I mastered the pieces I was supposed to play, I started improvising with the music, jazzing things up a bit. My teacher hated my doing this, and she tried to get me back on the straight and narrow by giving me more challenging parts to learn. Again, as soon as I mastered them, I'd begin to create and play variations on the themes, writing my own music. I learned I needed to do this; both playing and writing music unlocks a part of me that nothing else does—a creative part that helps make me whole.

Our church always had a worship band, and as soon as I was able, I played on Sundays with people of all ages. By high school, I was teaching myself to play other instruments. When we needed a drummer at church, my parents brought a drum kit as an early Christmas present. I practiced for two weeks before I felt comfortable playing the drums during a service.

By the time I graduated from high school, I had enough confidence in my musical ability to not fear the audience or what they'd think, but I still didn't have confidence or pride in *myself*. My fear of failure kept me down. Despite that handicap, I learned to lead teams of musicians, and this taught me a tremendous amount about being a competent leader. As I learned how to embrace everyone's individual creative genius and put them in a position to unlock their creativity, I learned more about how to run a business than anything I learned later from leadership books. God was prepping me how to read the room, take different people to work on one goal, and build them up to be a team.

I'd begun leading worship services at church when I was 15, and felt comfortable in front of a full church, singing, playing, or preaching. I literally had a key to the church and was leading worship at conferences by 16. By the time I was 17 or 18, I was sure of my path, and my vision had few boundaries. I knew I was going to be a well-known worship leader, traveling the world, and releasing albums of Christian music. There I was, on the stage, according to the lens I was looking through.

> "I don't tolerate any abuse of anyone"

But that was the problem. I saw through my own lens, not the one God used. It took more than 15 years for me to learn the difference.

I hadn't yet learned the many ways adversity can strike. I knew a string could break, or someone on your team could be in the wrong key—*that* I could handle. But I never expected that I couldn't make a living doing what I yearned to do, what I knew I was meant to do. My adversity became my self-inflicted, self-prophesied fear of failure. I lost sight of hope as every door closed in my face.

Throughout my twenties, I struggled. I was playing music around the world, but I wanted so much more. *What was wrong?* I kept asking myself. I thought I was experienced, charismatic, meant for the role, and I'd been told for years that I had a gift. But I didn't move past where I'd been when I was in high school. People were surpassing me, and I lost confidence as well as hope. If only I realized then that it wasn't failure that I was facing.

For years, I couldn't find a permanent church position, though I had plenty of part-time jobs leading worship. Finally, ten years ago, a church in Denver hired me onto its full-time staff. I moved there with my wife, Ashley, when she had just learned she was pregnant. We took it as a good omen: a new beginning for us all. I was now a full-time worship pastor and a father-to-be, and I saw nothing but good tidings ahead.

Over the first four months, the church membership doubled in size. People were talking about me, and they were happy about the work I was doing, as was I. Unfortunately, the lead pastor was insecure. He asked me to stay in a box, a limited role that didn't fit my vision for either the position or the church. I did my best for another month or two, but a few weeks before my daughter was born, the pastor fired me.

I was terrified and stunned. *What am I doing with my life?* I asked myself. I had failed, which in my mind meant I was also a failure. I couldn't envision any possible future. Fortunately, God was protecting me, and He showed me the path through His own lens. It took a while, though, before I could see my path clearly.

After our daughter was born, we moved back to Kansas City. I got a job working in construction, and Ashley began a cleaning business to help bring in the money we needed for our growing family. We were surviving but not getting ahead. I knew there must be something bigger in my future, but when you're working paycheck to paycheck, it's hard to set money aside to start something of your own. An opportunity arose from other people's bad fortune when Hurricane Ian devastated Florida in 2022. I headed to the Sunshine State to re-roof houses damaged in the hurricane. I knew I could build up a financial stake if I could work hard enough, for there was a tremendous unfilled need for workers.

I had never developed the ability to work really, incredibly hard, but I did so then. I learned how to push myself, to push through exhaustion, and to develop a "burn-the-ships" mentality. I slept in my car sometimes and continued to send money home, but I knew what was important was nailing down my future, not just nailing down another roof. I was *not* going to come home with my tail between my legs. That would have wiped us out financially, and it also would have buried me emotionally. I couldn't bear the thought of Ashley being disappointed.

When I look back at my early life, I can see I just went ahead and *did* things, and usually did them pretty well. I just didn't talk much about them or give myself any credit for a job (or a gig) well done. I never tried to be around successful people and learn from them.

Why? Of course I couldn't—I was a failure. At least, so went my mindset.

Though I began to see success and gain confidence, my fear didn't dissipate at first. When would the bottom drop out, I wondered, tiredly. But then I realized I was finding solutions, fixing problems, and managing people with empathy and good decision-making. Much of what I know about managing people comes from my experience managing musical groups and worship, but it's easily transferable to any workplace.

After five months in Florida, I was steadily asking myself, *Why am I not running my own business?* The timing was perfect, and it didn't take long to turn myself around once I reached that stage. I realized I could affect more people with what I could do with a business than I could by talking to them in church. As a business owner, I can say things that even a pastor can't say.

I had finally realized my true calling. Without looking back or hesitating, I founded Trusted Roofing with everything I had. Seven months after I started the company, I joined a mastermind. I wrote a $25,000 check I couldn't afford and haven't looked back. I have absolutely no regrets. I joined because I needed to attain what I thought were more lofty goals than I'd set for my business in the first few months. I knew I had to fix my head before I could grow my business.

As I worked with coaches and mentors, I began to articulate and demonstrate what I knew intuitively to be true: about hope, support, and kindness. I hit my new business' goals in just six months. My mindset was shifting. It wasn't very long before the path became clearer. Now that I was using the right lens, He showed me the way.

Since joining that mastermind, I've learned that building character and confidence takes time. If I'd become successful ten years earlier, I'd just have squandered the opportunities I created. I had to make *myself* successful before I could have a successful business—I had to first invest in myself and grow as a person. It boils down to one basic concept: *I had to allow myself to feel hopeful.*

As time passed, I've developed deeper empathy, which is something I consider more important than just success, and I reached a stage where I realized everybody couldn't be perfect. Whenever my team had a glitch, or maybe I even had to take a bit of a personal financial hit, instead of reacting, I'd encourage them and back them up. In business, this has served me well. I've developed more resiliency, and so has Trusted Roofing.

I've learned to build expectations and share the hope of high achievements with my staff, and at the same time accept their occasional failings with grace. They learn from their failures as I teach them to see themselves and their abilities as I do. Invariably, they realize I see them as individuals, as fully developed people with multiple dimensions, not just as employees. They're individuals with families, wonderful children, and amazing marriages. They realize I'm rooting for them in all aspects of their lives.

Yes, my business will make money for my family and positively affect their future. That is the reason I started the company. But by building my business culture in the manner I'm doing it, I can affect the present and future of all who work on my team. They will see holistic change in their lives, making more money but at the same time improving their relationships as they realize they're being supported in all these aspects. I want to see them be able to make huge, positive changes in their lives, including their personal relationships.

I don't tolerate any abuse of anyone—employees, managers, subcontractors, or clients. Traditional businesses don't behave with zero tolerance. They accept and justify abuse within the organization, usually with the excuse of the bottom line or lapses in management.

> " Never forget your team is your greatest asset. We treat people with respect. "

Of course, I delegate responsibility just like any other business owner, and I can't and won't try to manage everyone myself. While our company is not a traditional top-down bureaucracy, people still must take responsibility and make sure tasks are done the right way, by themselves or others. But I deeply care about how the management is done.

All employees hear this from me: "I brought you on because I believe you will thrive in this culture. But please understand that we don't tolerate yelling, even when someone has screwed up royally. There hasn't been any verbal abuse in this company, and there won't be. And if I hear of any, maybe we can have a conversation, and maybe you can make it right, but abuse is not acceptable for any reason. No matter what the offense might be, we treat people with respect."

Making that clear up front makes it so much easier for everyone to treat each other with respect. When they see how I operate, they see how I handle mistakes and lapses in judgment or performance, they can model that behavior themselves. Seeing my example helps them grasp our company culture. There is no shame, ever; instead we say, *How can we clean this up? How can we learn and grow from this?*

First and foremost, I get to know our people on a personal level, a place where I can speak into their lives, where I'm someone they listen to. The culture is about them—about people—not data. When it's money and data that matter most to your company, you're going to choose money over the relationship every time.

Trusted Roofing is not a traditional roofing company. To get new business, we don't go into neighborhoods and knock on doors, asking if we can give them quotes; instead, we train our people to network. We train them on how to use referral partners for new business, and we don't put money into traditional marketing practices, just a bare minimum into online advertising. We spend enough online money to give us a decent ranking and a legitimate hit on a search engine, but that's it. Our biggest goal is to train our people to network.

How do we build referral partners? With transparency.

Most of my team is made up of commissioned sales reps who theoretically work for me on a non-exclusive basis, but have made the choice to be exclusive, though I don't demand it. I pay exceptionally well—including a percentage of our profit—and I treat the staff equally well. I must be very transparent with our pricing so the sales reps know all our costs. They get to see the actual invoices from our suppliers and the subcontractors. They see every single cost, every single dollar.

In a way, I'm training my future competition. I'm transparent about all the other factors involved in the business, all the hassles and frustrations nobody talks about. I recently was tied up for three weeks on an insurance audit, for example. The insurance company made me want to bash my head against the wall every single day because of its stubbornly inane approach, and I shared what was happening with our team.

I'm prepared for the day when an employee may come to me and say, "You know what, Ryan? I think I want to start my own business, and I think this is the right thing for my family." Rather than being peeved, I can honestly respond, "You know what's involved, and if that's what you feel like doing, I'll support you. You ask me questions, I'll answer. I'll help you. I won't look at you as competition. I'm your friend still, and I'll still talk to you, and I'll still go to lunch with you."

I can nurture the hope they have for their futures and make sure I don't limit their vision to working for me forever.

Virtually all roofers use subcontractors for the actual roofing and gutter labor, and I do as well, hiring them for everything but cleanup and deliveries. In this industry, it's traditional that just about everyone nickel-and-dimes their subcontractors—their labor crew—and beats them down on price. I don't. Instead, I see them as my partners. If I don't have a crew to do the work, I don't have a roofing business. They're instrumental to our business, the core of what we do, so I don't play games with their money. I pay them every single week—on time—and never miss a payment.

I also want to invest in them, to make sure their businesses flourish, because I don't want them to live paycheck to paycheck, unable to buy the new truck they need when the old one is falling apart. I want them to succeed in every aspect of their lives, from their finances to their families. If my employees are successful, they'll help me succeed. Now I'm coaching my main subcontractors and asking them how they're doing financially and otherwise. We'll talk about pricing, and I ask questions such as, "Where do you feel like you're getting pinched, and where can we compromise?"

When my gutter guy came with a price for a certain gutter guard, I told him, "Jim, you need to charge more than that. I appreciate that you're giving me a good price, but you need to charge more to install that product. You're not going to set yourself up for success by charging the price you quoted. You could charge a little more and you'd still give me what I consider to be fair."

It's important that I'm being transparent with them. I tell them, "I want you to win, but also, I hold you accountable. You know when you screw something up, you need to go clean it up, but at the same time, I want you to build a business that's really successful as well, and I'd love to be your business partner this way for years to come."

I don't want to just burn through contractors and see who can do it the cheapest. It's okay to sacrifice a few dollars to build relationship capital. The more I build my business, the more relationships matter. I can't do it without them. They should succeed too, right?

*Why don't more people realize this?*

I truly don't understand. In most trades, the contractors are ruthless with their subcontractors; they see them as expendable and easily replaceable. I feel the opposite. The team we've built has been amazing, and I can easily put them up against anybody in Kansas City.

Maybe that's why we've been successful. The business is built to be all about relationships, and its success is the result of relationships. Rather than just hiring people and bringing warm bodies in to do a job, we're headhunting quality people for a long-term basis, people we get to know and help build up.

When we're networking strongly and deeply, it's possible to notice people running a different subcontracting business, a group that works the way we admire and appreciate, and say to them, "I truly admire the way you work and how you run your company. Will you talk with me about a possible switch to roofing? I'd like you to consider working with us at Trusted. I think you would be pleasantly surprised."

I've never had to put an ad out for a hiring position yet, though I'm always unofficially head-hunting. As we expand, I'm sure that will change, because I have some scaled-up ideas coming soon for national outreach. I'm filled with hope.

We're adapting the age-old tradecraft of roofing to the 21st century with the way we use and trust our people, and they use artificial intelligence to crunch and analyze data. We're finding ways to take "acts of God" out of most of the work we do, finding weather-proof and recession-proof work for our crews. Our competitors are relying on hailstorms, tornados, and other weather-driven events instead. As we add hope to this mixture of old and new, we're creating a new model for our business.

I admit to making errors. The $2,500 I spent to promote our company on grocery receipts has to be the dumbest money I ever wasted. I'm still refining my methods, and before I become any form of expert or consultant for pay, I intend to build my business from eight to nine figures.

> " We treat people with respect. "

To me, success means I'm building something that's bigger than me, with an equally bigger impact. I'm building a legacy. I know I need to consistently challenge myself by living outside my comfort zone to become a voice that really matters.

My family life has grown deeper and richer as I improved my mindset and the way I thought about myself and the world. I've learned to give to causes that break my heart. I don't believe I'm naïve when I say that seems to be a good battle cry for philanthropy.

Ashley and I are hoping to help break the cycle of the foster child system. We feel personally about the subject after caring for and hoping to adopt a child who came to us when he was five weeks old. When he was two, the courts ordered him back to his mother, though the social workers confirmed it would not be a good situation for him. When he was taken away, it was like a death in the family.

Children are not being cared for in the current setups, and they have no place bouncing around "in the system" as it exists. This is a situation where money alone could break the evil cycle of foster kids giving birth to another generation of foster children. Most experts agree that money in the right place will fix it. Social workers are overworked and underpaid, ignored when they shouldn't be, and, at the least, their wages should be doubled. Good foster parents could be found and trained.

My goal is to educate the church community on foster care. Churches can become a major part in the remaking of the foster system, and they're already beginning to become more involved through training, offering support, and supplying a variety of resources. I'd love to be the voice that connects those who are seeing results as they become involved in fostering, and help those who aren't doing as well. I also plan to put a good percentage of company profits into creating change at the government level and to finally abolish the current foster care system.

Improving the futures of potential foster children, keeping them out of a toxic system, and giving children hope: This is a legacy that Ashley and I hope to be able to leave. Improving the lives of my team members and their families, and instilling hope in *their* futures, is what we're already doing now.

The two legacies have one key factor in common: hope.

# ABOUT RYAN HILL

The business Ryan built from scratch 31 months ago has billed more than $17 million dollars since its founding, a remarkable feat for a man without investors, outside support, or past ownership experience. Not only has Trusted Roofing become a successful and profitable business in less than three years, it's built on a wholly reimagined business culture—one of hope, transparency, empathy, positive support, kindness, and shared responsibility. Ryan supports and trusts his teammates and subcontractors, and he encourages them to build their own profitable businesses, a rare trait in a contractor. To him, people are his greatest asset, and they are to be nurtured and appreciated.

As a man of deep faith, Ryan has led worship and played music in churches since he was 15 years old, including a period as worship pastor for a Denver church. He practices what he preaches in every aspect of his life. When he realized he could affect more people with a business than through church, he overcame his fear of failure and founded his unique roofing company.

After a painful experience fostering and losing a child who should never have returned into the system, Ryan and his wife, Ashley, hope to help break the cycle of the foster child system through working with and educating churches and their congregations. They hope to leave a legacy of giving children hope and keeping them out of toxic situations, finding supportive, positive homes for them, and a better future.

Ryan was a musical prodigy, teaching himself to play many instruments and improvise music from middle school on. He was raised playing sports and intense board and card games with his family. He still loves sports and games, and continues to play both whenever possible, hoping his three kids will be his future golf partners as he and they age. He and his family live in Lee's Summit, Missouri.

 www.trustedkc.com

 ryanleehill85

 ryanleehill85

# Awaken the Greatness Within You

## BRENDA PETRILLO

have never been one to play small.

Not in how I love. Not in how I rise. Not in how I fight to reclaim my life.

Every countless challenge I've faced has offered me a binary choice: Stay in the familiar, silent, stuck, small, or take the hard right turn that will bring clarity, courage, and change. I refuse to let fear chain me to a life that isn't mine. You must stop waiting for someone to save you and save yourself.

I am not a tidy success story, but women don't need more perfection; we need more permission to rise messily, late, and loudly. My willingness to be transparent about my arduous journey gives me strength and is what I share with my co-authors. I'm not afraid to share the good and the bad because there is strength in vulnerability.

I have had days when I've built businesses and buried secrets. I've led global change initiatives by day and cried myself to sleep in silence. I've been called powerful and made to feel powerless. However, every version of me contributed to the creation of a seasoned corporate executive and a strategic reinvention coach. I didn't rise by accident. I grew because I had to, and then I chose to rise even higher as a visionary entrepreneur, building businesses that reflect both purpose and power.

I like to say I received an assignment before I was born. My mother, Sally, had fought and won an extraordinary battle with bipolar disorder and schizophrenia. She spent two years in a catatonic state at a psychiatric center.

One day, my mother broke through her catatonia and asked another patient for a puff of their cigarette. Not long after, she was well enough to come home. She surprised my dad when almost her first words to him after coming out of her catatonic state were, "I want to have another baby," despite the fact my two brothers were already teenagers. And she did, at age 36.

My mother's decision created repercussions in my life that I'm sure she never expected. As early as I can remember, I felt it was my responsibility to save her from her mental illness and make her life better. Fortunately, my father's strength anchored my life as well as my mother's health for the first decade of my life. He loved us both unconditionally, and he stood by her through the ups and downs of her mental illness. I learned the value of love and perseverance from both my parents; it was the foundation for much of what I took into my adult life. Their passion for one another and their determination to hold our family together taught me never to give up, no matter what the odds.

Mom never let her mental illness stop her from achieving. She wrote more than 200 songs, with thirteen of those copyrighted and four published. She worked with some of the biggest names in music. Her initiative and resourcefulness were incredible. She chased her purpose with a fire that never quit, and her fire lit something inside of me, too. Mom showed me what it meant to be fearless in the face of adversity and taught me how to dream with a wild, unapologetic heart.

When my dad was diagnosed with amyotrophic lateral sclerosis (ALS), or Lou Gehrig's disease, I was only nine, and it devastated all of us. My mother reversed roles and became his pillar of strength. I watched her nurse him with a level of tenderness and devotion that equaled the years of loving care he'd given her. He was gone just nine months after his diagnosis, and the foundation of my world shifted.

After my dad died, grief and grit filled our home. I watched mom struggle to keep food on the table, saw her bury herself under the blankets for days, and lived through the trauma of her seizures, suicide attempts, and breakdowns.

She never gave up on raising me to the best of her ability, and I knew I was the center of her world, but I often felt that I was raising us both. I became much more than just a daughter. I'd inherited parts of my new role from my dad. I became her confidante, her companion, and far too often her caregiver. I tried to be strong for her every day because I knew she was trying hard to hold it together. It was a tremendous burden for a child, but I wouldn't have had it any other way. I knew we both needed to survive her challenges. I loved her and still do.

Coping with the constant ups and downs and unpredictability of her illness drained and marked me. I wasn't the easiest teenager to be around. I was starting to find my voice and acting out in all the usual ways, such as drinking alcohol and being a little rebellious.

The ongoing financial struggle we had after my dad died was another key stressor in my young life, and it profoundly shaped my values and carved something unshakeable into me. I vowed never to put myself in a position where I had to depend on anyone else for stability or financial survival. That commitment became a defining part of my identity, shaping my ambition and catapulting me forward. It fueled my drive to build an independent and secure life. I didn't just want success; I needed it like oxygen.

Growing up in the Adirondacks, I knew I wanted more than what I saw around me. Of course, the traditional exit strategy was college. I wasn't an exceptional student, and higher education felt financially and academically out of reach. When I was old enough to consider college, I was too rebellious and distracted by my struggles.

Despite my promises to myself, I wasn't on target to reach any of my goals. At age 25, I was broke, divorced, paying a mortgage that cost more than half of my salary, juggling two dead-end jobs, and making barely $13,000 a year. A moment of clarity hit me: *I was going nowhere fast.*

Something inside me shifted. I remembered what I had intuitively realized when I watched my mother struggle on her own: *I am meant for more, but the only person who can change my circumstances is me.* That realization marked a turning point in my life.

I took a leap, landed a temp job at a local phone company, and got my first break. I worked as a customer care consultant in the call center, which I thoroughly enjoyed. My boss, Susan Harrington, saw something in me and gave me a chance to work on an Information Technology (IT) project. This single opportunity lit a spark that would ignite the rest of my life.

Soon, I was sitting down with a 5-by-7-inch yellow-lined pad, scribbling out a plan. My goal was simple yet ambitious: I aimed to earn $100,000 by the time I was 30, less than five years away.

My education became something far more focused than a general college education. I gained knowledge through real-world experiences, earned industry certifications, and built a foundation of self-taught expertise that fueled my success. Though I eventually came within a semester of earning a bachelor's degree from Arizona State University, my most important education was forged in the trenches, leading complex, multimillion-dollar initiatives, cross-functional teams, and navigating high-stakes dynamics of corporate America.

Six months shy of my 30th birthday, I was in California, leading a team of information security professionals at a salary of $105,000 per year for one of the world's most renowned software companies. I met my goal! That moment wasn't just about hitting a number; it was about proving to myself that I could create the life I had dared to dream about. That decision to bet on myself changed everything, and it set me on a successful career trajectory that has taken me around the world, working for Fortune 100 and 500 companies, living in China and Singapore, and building a thriving career I not only enjoyed but took fierce pride in.

While I climbed the corporate ladder, privately, my life painted a different picture and took much longer to make the same switch. I was drowning in toxic, manipulative, abusive love—or what I thought was love.

> "Success is a journey, not a destination."

I got married at 21, in love and full of hope. My first husband didn't start as a monster, but it didn't take long before I was walking on eggshells, bracing for the next rage or the next punishment.

Despite my denial that my marriage was destructive to *me*, I knew I couldn't bring a child into such a dangerous environment. After he threatened me and our unborn child, I had a secret abortion. It was one of the most challenging decisions I've made, but it was the right one for me and the life I was carrying.

One day, in the middle of a fight, he grabbed me by the throat and lifted me off the ground. My legs dangled. His cousin's stepdaughter, just a toddler, stood frozen, watching.

I knew if I didn't leave, I might not make it. I took two weeks to gather my courage and ask my husband for what I euphemistically called "a break." When he agreed, I packed his bags and handed them to him as he walked out the door. The next day, I filed for a restraining order and divorce.

Why didn't I leave sooner? Why did I stay at all? Those are the questions I asked myself for too many years as I continued in a series of toxic relationships, each one as destructive as the last, each one teaching me what love is not. On the surface, everything looked perfect, but behind closed doors, I was navigating the chaos of abusive relationships that few knew existed. Years later, I found myself married again. This time, to a man whose charm was so convincing, I didn't see the trap until I was already inside. He was brilliant, handsome, and a clinically diagnosed narcissist who gaslighted me, twisted my reality, and made me question my strength and sanity. When police arrested him for luring a minor in a sting operation, I stayed. For five more years, I endured constant emotional abuse.

I hid everything—his arrest, his guilty plea, his registered status. I told no one, except my best friend and his family. It felt like an undeniable weight I carried alone.

Why did I stay yet again? Because I thought I could fix him, just like I thought I could fix everyone else. That burning need to heal the broken wasn't new—it was in my DNA. But healing doesn't come from fixing others. It comes from reclaiming yourself. When I realized that, something shifted inside me.

It was like every emotional wound I'd ever carried—the abandonment, the abuse, the bruises you couldn't see—suddenly healed at once. Not perfectly. Not prettily. But powerfully.

In a split second, I didn't just feel my worth—I saw it, standing outside myself, radiant and undeniable. For the first time in my life, I understood:

- I was never meant to fix anyone.
- I wasn't broken; I was becoming.

When I realized all of that and the implications, I threw the television remote control, not in a rage, but in release.

And with a voice that shook with the force of my awakening, I spoke the words that changed everything: GET OUT!

And, just like that, I chose me.

If you've been waiting for a permission slip to choose yourself, THIS IS IT! You don't need anyone else's blessing to rise. You don't need more reasons to leave what's breaking you. YOU are the reason. If you need someone to hand you that permission slip, let me be the one to place it firmly into your hands.

After that epiphany, I focused on myself and became someone with whom a genuinely great person would want to partner. I created space for myself first. I didn't just focus on the relationship I wanted; I focused on the woman I was becoming. I didn't manifest a hero to rescue me. I manifested a partner who could meet me where I stood strong, sovereign, and ready.

And that's when Steve showed up. A professional firefighter, no less. A real-life hero by trade, but by the time he found me, I didn't need saving. I needed someone who could stand in the fire with me.

We've been married for fifteen years, and every day, I'm reminded of what's possible when you heal, choose yourself, and open yourself up to the relationship and joy you deserve. Life constantly challenges us. I don't define my happiness by being with Steve; instead, he enhances the joy and contentment I create within myself.

Before I met him, I had stopped dancing in the living room. As a child, I danced freely, especially when my dad was alive or my mom had a good day. But somewhere along the way, I lost that part of myself. Meeting Steve didn't give it back to me—finding myself did.

Now, I dance in the living room all the time, music blaring, spirit soaring, and celebrating not just the relationship we've built, but the life I've fought for, the woman I've become, and the road I traveled to get here.

Dancing for me is gratitude in motion. Gratitude for my happiness, freedom, and the fierce, unstoppable version of me that rose from the ashes. Happiness and fulfillment are never about titles, paychecks, or even love itself. They're about what those things bring: security, comfort, peace, and joy.

Transformation starts with choices—sometimes small, sometimes seismic. You must choose to believe you deserve more, to bet on yourself, to choose to step toward the life you envision, even when the path ahead terrifies you. It's never one choice; It's choosing yourself repeatedly.

And every brave, messy, heartbroken, hope-fueled choice I made shaped me into the current version of myself: A woman who no longer chases approval and stands firmly in her worth.

One of the most significant changes in my life has been learning to trust my intuition. It had always been there, but for years, I silenced it. The first time I was married, I knew deep down I shouldn't have gone through with it. The signs were there. The voice inside me whispered, "Don't do it." But I told myself it was easier to move forward than to pull the brake. These weren't grand affairs with hundreds of guests or showers of gifts. They were quiet, small weddings. There were no fairy tale moments, just me convincing myself that love, or the idea of it, was enough. Even though I was only ten years old when I lost my father, I believed I knew what he would have wanted for me to hold out for a man who was worthy of his little girl. And before Steve, none of them were.

Learning to trust my intuition didn't happen overnight. I slowly reclaimed the voice I had buried under fear and loneliness. My intuition isn't just a whisper; it's a force. It influences every decision I make, and I trust it without hesitation. It is the compass that keeps me true to myself, no matter how loud the world gets.

Today, I don't live in the past. I don't carry regret like a heavy cloak around my shoulders. I have compassion for the woman I was—a woman who was trying to navigate life, find love, and heal in the only ways she knew how. I've forgiven her because she deserves forgiveness and grace. And I've forgiven those who hurt me, too. Not for them. For me. Forgiveness isn't about excusing what happened; it's about freeing your heart to create a future that isn't chained to an old story. Holding on to pain keeps you tethered to the past. Letting it go sets you free.

Recognizing the most influential people in my life is integral to understanding my journey. And here's the irony: They aren't just the people who loved me; they're also the ones who didn't. Those relationships, as painful as they were, created the unstoppable woman I am today.

My philosophy is simple: Regret, forgiveness, and growth are choices. Every decision, misstep, and moment I wished had gone differently led me to a life that feels aligned, joyful, and mine.

I dislike the word "failure." It feels too final, too narrow, and too small to define the whole arc of a life like mine. Life isn't a pass/fail test; it's a series of lessons. What some people call failures, I see as invitations to grow, pivot, and evolve. That mindset shaped how I approach adversity and setbacks. Success isn't just about winning; it's about how you rise when things fall apart.

> " Legacy isn't what you leave behind. It's what you spark in others while you're still here "

I've started things and not finished them. I didn't complete my bachelor's degree, which many might consider a failure. My decision to focus on non-traditional education set me on a path to prove that a piece of paper doesn't define success. I've built up successful businesses and a thriving career, achieved multi-seven-figure earnings, and worked for some of the world's most respected organizations, all without a college degree. The world's definitions of success and failure don't have to be yours.

Failure isn't about what didn't work; it's about how you faced the wreckage, learned from it, and determined your next move. I've proven to myself that no matter what falls apart, I can and will make the bold move, because even in chaos, I know how to lead the board.

When I was younger, success was simple: the sprawling mansion I sketched in art class and a life that felt grand and far removed from the small-town reality in which I grew up. It wasn't that I didn't love my hometown, but I knew it wasn't where my dreams would thrive. Back then, success meant escaping the familiar, getting a good job, and building a life that looked impressive from the outside. For a while, I chased that version of success relentlessly.

The job I landed at 29½ was working at a Fortune 500 company, earning six figures, managing a team, and occupying a high-rise office with a window. I lived in a cute apartment and felt like I'd made it. That version of success—title, salary, and independence—felt tangible and so validating.

Then, 9/11 hit, and the information technology industry hit a massive downturn. I wasn't just watching the layoffs happen; I was helping to lead them, until one day, I found myself laid off, too. I was devastated. It was a wake-up call I never saw coming. I realized painfully that I had tied my worth to the tangibles—the job, the income, and the title; but they were just achievements. But when it all disappeared, I had to face a truth I'd been running from: the external markers of success might make you feel seen, but they'll never make you feel whole.

At 54, my definition of success has evolved into something more profound and intangible. Today, success is about the life I've built, the peace I feel, the love I share with my husband, and the joy of being surrounded by true friends who treat me with kindness, respect, and genuine care. It's about living in a beautiful home that serves as a sanctuary, filled with love, laughter, and our beloved poodles. Most of all, it's about knowing that I'm at a place in life where I want for nothing. Not because I have everything, but because I finally became everything I once needed.

Success is not a fixed destination. It's a moving force, constantly evolving, continually expanding, just like me. I am and always will be a lifelong learner, reaching for the next thing, driven by the little girl who saw her mother struggle and vowed to create a different life. That motivation still fuels me, but it's no longer about proving myself to the world. It's about fulfilling my purpose and helping others reach their full potential.

If you ask me today if I've succeeded, I'd say yes and no. Yes, I am successful. I've built a life I'm proud of, filled with gratitude, joy, and calm. But success is something you never fully grasp. Striving, learning, and growing make life meaningful. Success is a journey, not a destination.

Success is about balance: striving for greatness while appreciating where I am. It's about joy, resilience, and the ability to create a life that feels whole and complete. It's ever-changing, and it's a privilege to continue defining it as I grow.

The day I fulfilled a promise to my older brother, Bobby, changed me forever. Bobby was the kind of soul who lit up every room he entered—charismatic, funny, handsome, and heartbreakingly human. His struggles with addiction never erased his kindness or his beautiful spirit.

I had promised Bobby he would not die alone. When I arrived at his bedside, Bobby was in a coma, but somehow, he knew I was there. He rallied for a brief, miraculous moment, looked straight at me, and said, "I love you, sis." Those were his last words. When he slipped back into a coma, the doctors turned to me to make the decision I knew was coming.

That night, I held his hand as he took his last breath, overwhelmed by a profound, almost sacred peace. It was one of the most extraordinary experiences of my life. Helping him transition to the other side felt like the mirror image of a mother bringing new life into the world. It was a moment that shifted me, not just emotionally, but spiritually. That experience planted a seed inside me that eventually grew into a deep passion for helping others through profound life transitions. It led me to become an End-of-Life Doula, holding sacred space for those crossing over, and for their loved ones who stay behind. Loss came in waves after that. Two years later, I lost my mother. A decade later, I lost my brother Michael to the same disease that took our father, ALS. Each goodbye left a scar. But each scar also cracked me open in new, beautiful ways. Because with every loss, I found another part of myself.

After Bobby passed, something wild and unexpected stirred in me—an undeniable urge to create. I walked into an art supply store and spent $500 on brushes, paint, and canvas. I didn't know what I was doing—I just knew I had to do it. To my surprise, I discovered a raw, untamed talent for painting. Local galleries and bistros featured my abstract paintings and resin art. People commissioned pieces. They hung my art in their homes. And for the first time in a long time, I realized: Grief didn't just break me. It helped me grow into a fuller, richer version of who I was meant to become. Now, creativity flows through every part of my life—not just in the art I create, but in the lives I help others design as well. Through coaching, healing work, every word I write, and every space I hold. Healing became not just a personal journey, but a sacred calling. As a Reiki Master, ThetaHealer, and Quantum Healing Hypnosis Technique (QHHT) practitioner, I discovered new ways to help others release pain, reconnect with their inner wisdom, and realign with their most authentic selves. I don't just offer traditional coaching. I offer transformational, soul-level healing—helping women rise not just emotionally, but energetically, spiritually, and creatively.

Whether it's helping a woman break free from toxic cycles, guiding her back to her intuition, or holding sacred space as she heals from unseen wounds, I bring every part of myself to the work I do. Because I know firsthand: sometimes the most significant losses crack us open, so the light inside can finally escape.

As I write this chapter, I've considered a few significant moments. One was the launch of my coaching career, when I attended a

Mastermind event featuring Dean Graziosi and Tony Robbins. Without preparation, I was invited to share my story on stage in front of 150 people. For years, I had visualized myself speaking on stage, and suddenly, there I was for the first time. It was humbling and empowering. Soon, I found myself at the Mastermind headquarters, standing in a multi-million-dollar recording studio, filming a welcome video and a sales talk for my business. When I left the studio, I broke into what Oprah would call an ugly cry of overwhelming gratitude and pride. I realized how far I had come and how every decision and challenge had led me to that moment.

> " My decision to focus on non-traditional education set me on a path to prove that a piece of paper doesn't define success. "

The legacy I hope to leave isn't a plaque or generational wealth. Legacy is about the ripple effect on how I can continue to inspire and transform lives long after I'm gone. My legacy is the movement I aim to create—a movement that empowers people, especially women, to realize their full potential. Legacy isn't what you leave behind. It's what you spark in others while you're still here.

I want my legacy to be a beacon of hope for those who feel stuck in toxic cycles, whether personal or professional. I remind my clients that healing is possible, and they can rebuild their self-worth and design lives that reflect their purpose, potential, and undeniable power. Everyone deserves to live their life with joy, freedom, and deep fulfillment, and I'm here to help them claim it. Through my coaching, books, speaking engagements, and retreats, I aim to help others recover and thrive far more quickly than it took me. My vision is to help people not only survive their hardships but thrive in their lives, build fulfilling relationships and careers, and realize they are far more capable than they ever believed.

Humor and transparency effectively serve as therapy when life feels heavy. I've learned to laugh and encourage others to do the same, even in the darkest moments. My openness and willingness to discuss my experiences, no matter how personal they may seem, have been my way of connecting with others and finding meaning in adversity. It's a reminder that we're all human and face struggles. I want to inspire others to talk about their struggles by being open about mine.

My legacy is also about creating physical and virtual spaces where transformation happens. I want my retreats to be life-changing, my books to sit on coffee tables as constant reminders of resilience and possibility, and my words to echo in conversations among friends, families, and communities. While many of my events welcome corporate leaders and successful entrepreneurs, they are especially designed for women from all walks of life, those who are rising from setbacks, navigating reinvention, or simply ready to build something meaningful on their own terms.

My legacy is growing and evolving, and I have many years to finish shaping it. What sets it apart from so many others is that it's not just about the result; it's about the lives I can change along the way.

Titles, trophies, or timelines don't measure a legacy. My legacy will be every woman who chooses to prioritize herself.

Legacy is in every heart that beats louder because you refused to stay silent.

It's in every fire sparked by the flames you refused to let die.

You don't leave a legacy by living a perfect life. You leave a legacy by rising bloody, brilliant, and unbreakable and daring others to rise with you.

And that is how you set the whole damn world on fire.

# ABOUT BRENDA PETRILLO

Brenda Petrillo is a Strategic Reinvention Coach, women's leadership mentor, and unapologetic force of nature committed to helping high-achieving women turn life pivots into launch pads, reclaim their voice, and build lives that reflect their power, purpose, and potential.

With over 25 years of experience leading enterprise transformation, people-centered change, and high-impact strategy across Fortune 500 companies, Brenda brings both executive credibility and profound personal wisdom to every client she serves. She knows firsthand what it takes to rise because she's done it, again and again.

After surviving decades of emotionally abusive relationships, including the grip of narcissistic partners, Brenda hit a breaking point that became her breakthrough. She rebuilt her life from the inside out, healing wounds that once held her back, reclaiming her voice, and stepping into her highest calling: to help other women do the same, but in far less time.

Through her signature *Rise and Launch Method*™, she helps women turn adversity into advantage and reinvention into a roadmap for building lives filled with clarity, confidence, and lasting impact.

As the founder of **Anew Phoenix Rising, LLC**, Brenda leads transformational coaching programs, immersive retreats, and ethical AI business accelerators that empower women not to bounce back, but to boldly business what's next, on their terms.

She lives in Arizona with her husband, Steve, the man who honors her fire and dances with her in the living room. Together, they embody what's possible when healing meets wholeness and when a woman finally decides to rise.

 www.anewphoenixrising.com

 brendapetrillo

 BrendaLynnPetrillo

 @anewphoenixrising

 @anewphoenixrising

# God Directs...
# Pay Attention

## CARY CLAYBORN

You should know four things about me right up front.

First, I am a child of God. Second, I'm a reluctant writer who agreed to write a chapter in this anthology only if I could give glory to God. Third, I have been at Ground Zero for some of the most important events happening during my lifetime. And fourth, as my title suggests, I have been paying attention over the past five to six years as God directed me to amazing new heights and connectivity through dreams, visions, messages, and clarity.

When I reflect on my life as a whole—where I've been at certain times, what I've done, whom I've met—I believe I've been the Forrest Gump of Harrison, Arkansas. When I reflect specifically on the past recent years, I realize God's hand has been directing me. The more I've paid attention, the more my heart has been able to confirm that suffering leads to growth and to my witness and support of others.

In this chapter, I'll share spiritual lessons and some of the serendipitous experiences that accompany them. And yes, later I'll share how I learned to pay attention to God. Please know that this chapter comes from my own heart and is not academically founded, meaning that I'm not a seminary graduate, nor am I a pastor or minister, nor do I pretend that my insight is gospel. The wonderful thing about being a child and follower of God is that we can always grow and learn from the Bible, from others, and from prayer. It doesn't seem to matter how old we are, and there is certainly no correlation to our intelligence, success, or wealth.

My life has been a kaleidoscope of unique experiences. After graduating from the U. S. Military Academy (USMA) at West Point in 1986, I was stationed in West Germany during the Cold War. My first mission as an Air Defense platoon leader was to defend the East German communist border at a critical part of the border called the Fulda Gap.

I've kept a picture of me sitting in a tent on maneuvers, holding up Tom Clancy's book, *Red Storm Rising*, which was published that same year. The novel told the all-too-terrifying (and feasible) story of the Soviet Union plowing into Western Europe through the Fulda Gap. I performed well in that role and subsequently became a general's aide-de-camp to two different brigadier generals, both of whom were West Point grads and Vietnam veterans. I had business in Berlin just before The Wall fell, my first Forrest Gump moment, and suddenly I could simply drive across the once heavily guarded and dangerous border. The contrast between the haves and have-nots was stark in Eastern Europe; I shared an emotional outpouring with thousands of people on the Freedom Trains who kissed free ground for the first time in more than 30 years.

My five-year military commitment was up in 1991, and I left the Army and pursued medical sales in the cardiology field. I'd never done sales before, unless you factor keeping generals happy as sales work, but my West Point pre-med degree and the master's degree in science management I earned while I was in Germany were good background for the medical aspects of the work.

In 1993, I found out that I was pretty good at sales when I closed the first million-dollar contract in the history of my company, Cordis, within four months of joining the company. I flipped the Oklahoma territory, one of the worst-performing territories, to one of the best. My second Forrest Gump moment was connected to that job: I'd been in the Alfred P. Murrah Federal Building in April 1995, two weeks before the terrorist explosion that demolished it. I was getting a Veterans Administration loan for a house, so I'd been in that exact spot and felt personally affected by the bomb that killed 168 people and injured hundreds more.

A year later, I moved to Dallas-Fort Worth and began training to teach minimally invasive heart surgery with Heartport, my favorite medical sales job of my career. Soon Johnson & Johnson bought both the cardiology and heart surgery companies and offered to move me to New Jersey, but I decided to follow a fellow West Pointer's advice and move into money management.

I traded my scrubs for a suit and tie when I joined AllianceBernstein in 2001, which put me in Manhattan close to ground zero on 9/11. I was in Midtown when the Twin Towers fell, and massive crowds of New Yorkers and I watched in horror on big screens at the base of the General Motors building, which was home to *The Early Show*.

The next day, 9/12, was also significant for me because I suffered a major concussion playing touch football in Central Park. I landed on my head catching a pass while trying to avoid actor Kevin Bacon, who was throwing frisbees next to our game.

Speaking of celebrities, I have had the opportunity to meet dozens of actors, entertainers, professional athletes, singers, and other well-known people, whether attending black tie events in Hollywood, playing in celebrity golf tournaments, networking with them, or by just avoiding running into them, as I did with Mr. Bacon.

In retrospect, I deeply appreciate that God led me to these unique experiences which all equate to the Forrest Gump reference, but in my most recent years, I've also realized that none of it matters. My realigned ranking of importance are my relationship with God, my family (wife, daughter, parents, sister, nephews), my friends and close colleagues, my fellow humans, and my own hobbies (travel, golf, scuba). I suspect that most people struggle as I do to put our priorities in the correct order!

Now that I'm in my sixties, you would think that I'd be preparing for my so-called golden years, but when I finally learned how to pay attention to God, I began moving further from the notion of retirement. I know firsthand that if you're sincere in following God's will for you, He wants you to love Him and your neighbor, as the Bible suggests. When you do, every dimension and aspect of your life will improve. Personally, I have seen my bandwidth expand as God has placed several new opportunities in front of me, all of which are founded in faith and designed to help and support others.

My hometown is in the Ozark Mountains of Arkansas, where I had a middle-American, almost boringly normal upbringing. Like many from the South, I publicly professed my faith in Jesus Christ when I was around 10 years old, so I've considered myself a Christian my whole life. Accepting Christ and saying you are a Christian has very little to do with being a Christian, following Christ, or your walk with Christ. For me, my walk took shape only recently.

In high school, I was both athletic and a good student, ranked seventh in my class of 215. In track and field, I was All-State in the high and long jump, setting our school record for the high jump at six feet, nine inches (I'm six feet tall). My basketball skills were better; I led the Harrison Goblins in scoring during my junior and senior years, scoring 41 points once and in the upper-30s often. I was the only person I knew in my high school who didn't drink; I lived up to my dad's expectations and his example.

Attending the American Legion Boys State in my junior year, I learned about the U.S. Military Academy at West Point (USMA). Our high school counselor told me that a few Harrison High graduates had attended the other military academies, but none had ever attended West Point. The possibility of becoming the first appointee from our school intrigued my competitive spirit and my sense of adventure.

I was honored to receive nominations from both Arkansas senators and my local congressman, and by December of my senior year, I was accepted at both West Point and the Air Force academies. I chose USMA. As a walk-on, I led the junior varsity basketball team in scoring during most games and was promoted to the varsity squad by my sophomore year. After practicing throughout the off-season, I

" Suffering leads to growth. "

was burnt out, so instead I joined the Black Knights, the competitive sport parachute team, plus the Scuba Club, the Mountaineering Club, and I went to northern warfare training in Alaska. Skydiving with The Black Knights was fun, wild, and rewarding, though I did have a few incidents, including breaking my coccyx one year and slamming into the ground from 70 feet up the next year. Following graduation from West Point, I attended Army Airborne School to get my wings, which were the last jumps I've made... so far.

The Class of 1986 (with the motto *Courage Never Quits!*) had its fair share of people earning Army rank, including four-star Gen. (Ret.) Joe Martin (former Vice Chief of Staff of the U.S. Army) and four-star Gen. (Ret.) Dan Hokanson (former Chief, National Guard Bureau), but my class has been labeled three times over the years for different reasons: Business Class, Philanthropic Class, and Political Class.

It started with three stellar businessmen: Joe DePinto (current 20-year CEO of 7-Eleven), Steve Cannon (9-year CEO/President of Mercedes-Benz USA, then 8-year CEO of AMB), and Tony Guzzi (current 21-year chair/CEO of $15B+ EMCOR). Not just these three, but more than twenty other classmates have served as CEOs of various companies including Doug Black (11-year chair/CEO of SiteOne Landscape Supply), who was our running back and one of the nation's leading rushers during our junior and senior years when we beat Navy both years and won the 1984 Cherry Bowl and the 1985 Peach Bowl. The "Business" label is fair, but there are other USMA grads who have served as CEOs for other very large companies, including Procter & Gamble and Johnson & Johnson.

However, when one of our classmates, John McHugh, died of a suicide bomber in Kabul Afghanistan, Joe/Steve/Tony raised funds for the McHugh family with a golf tournament at West Point, then formed the Johnny Mac Soldiers Fund (JMSF, www.johnnymac. org), a non-profit led by classmate MaryEllen Picciuto. The founding board of directors (BOD) included six classmates and the deceased older brother, Jim McHugh. I joined the BOD in the second year and served for four years. JMSF has raised more than $50 million in 10 years, providing almost $40 million in scholarships to children of our nation's fallen or disabled warriors. Our "Philanthropic" label has been fully earned, as no class in West Point's history has done anything like this.

On the JMSF BOD was Dave Urban, a lobbyist who helped President Trump get elected to his first term. Then Dave helped put chess pieces in place to move 1986 Classmate Mike Pompeo from the CIA to Secretary of State and 1986 Classmate Mark Esper from Secretary of the Army to Secretary of Defense under Trump. There have never been two West Pointers in a presidential cabinet before, much less two classmates. We had eight classmates in Trump's first administration. Even 1986 Class President, Roger Carstens, stepped into the role of Special Envoy for Hostage Affairs, where he so effectively served in the role that President Biden kept him in place for his entire term. The "Political" label is fully earned and it's unlikely to ever be replicated.

When I was 30, I took up golf and it quickly became a passion, feeding both my competitive spirit and my love of travel. I have played almost 800 different golf courses across 45 states and 17 different countries. I've been to all 50 states while most of my global travel to 55 countries was before golf. My goal is to play a thousand different courses in all 50 states and in many more countries. As a bonus, I've found golf to be a great judge of character, which is important to me in every aspect of my volunteer and professional work.

Golf helps me evaluate people three ways:

*Integrity.* It's all too easy to cheat in golf. You're expected to referee yourself without any outside supervision, which is one of the aspects of golf I love. Undercounting strokes and sneakily relocating balls are just two ways people cheat with impunity.

*Emotional stability.* It's so easy to become upset and lose control of your emotions; the game of golf is unforgiving, and one slightly bad swing can lead to a ball landing in a hazard or out of bounds, or, embarrassingly, dribbling off the tee. In such circumstances, even professional golfers sometimes lose their cool. We amateurs are tested multiple times each round, and it's sometimes hard to hide your emotions in front of the other members of your foursome.

*Intestinal fortitude.* Some golfers have the unique ability to maintain fluidity and rhythm on a tee box after having a mortifying experience of a horrendous hole, where you hooked the ball into the woods, hit it in the water, and/or shanked it so badly you almost hit a playing companion. Intestinal fortitude is the management of your physical, emotional, and spiritual self, allowing you to get up on the next tee box and flush all of that out of your mind and hit the ball down the fairway with a free, relaxed swing.

Why is that important? Because I could do business with someone for a year or even longer and not know their character. If I play one round of golf with them, I will know enough of their integrity, emotional stability, and intestinal fortitude (plus their good humor, sportsmanship, and generosity of spirit) to decide whether I want to do business with them. There is no other way to spend four hours with someone and learn so much about them.

While playing with a professional acquaintance, I called a stroke on myself because my club brushed the back of a bunker. My playing partner said it didn't happen because he'd watched my swing, but I knew my club had touched. He later introduced me to a group of people as "the highest-integrity guy he'd ever met." I gained two clients from that introduction, though I'd had no intention of impressing anyone but myself.

Ideally, travel and golf are two things you can enjoy throughout your entire life. My right knee was replaced over 18 years ago and then my left knee was replaced in 2024, and as a result, I finally have full use of both legs for the first time in more than 20 years. I pray that God has many years to challenge me spiritually, mentally, and physically, so that I can continue to represent the best possible version of myself.

Speaking of golf, I once accidentally hit actor Gary Sinise in the back with a golf ball playing in an American Film Institute celebrity golf tournament. It was yet another serendipitous Gump-related incident that created a unique interaction. To be fair, it was a glancing blow that ricocheted off a tree, and I apologized at the end of the tournament. I'm very grateful for Mr. Sinise's support of veterans and for his outstanding characterization as Lieutenant Dan in *Forrest Gump*. There is a scene in the movie where Forrest and Lieutenant Dan are not having any luck catching shrimp, and Lieutenant Dan says, "Where the hell is this God of yours?"

Forrest narrates, "It's funny that Lieutenant Dan said that, because right then God showed up." The wind starts blowing and a sudden hurricane wipes out all the shrimp boats except for theirs.

I've personally discovered that God shows up and gives you messages or clues as long as you're aware and paying attention. It happens all the time in the most amazing ways. Sure, you can call them coincidences and fate, but I prefer to call it *faith*. The closer I'm able to align myself with my purpose and God's will for me, the more I'm able to see and pick up on these small signs. I'm even able to embrace the suffering which invariably lead to the direction and the opportunities that God has planned for me.

Let me describe to you some of the key spiritual happenings that have taken place recently and have convinced me that God directs our lives.

In mid-2019, I coordinated a series of meetings with thought leaders on behalf of a start-up business. When the person I was helping suddenly turned on me and tried to damage my reputation within my network, I was caught off guard and felt pain and anxiety. One day I prayed aloud, repeating hundreds of times, "God, please take this out of my head and out of my heart." That night God visited me in a vivid dream and explained that person's circumstances, why the issues were taking place, and exactly what to do about it. I woke up at peace, knowing how to handle the situation. In the end, my reputation remained intact and everything was resolved. Most importantly, I realized that I could turn over any burden to God not just through faith, but through trust.

> "When I'm aligned with God, what happens is God's plan for my life."

The next year, I was fighting my way through a demoralizing and unjust situation at work. At that same time, I hosted a father and son for lunch, but the son was in the middle of a 21-day water-only fast. He explained how the body adjusts and said fasting gave him spiritual clarity. His father, Daniel, also routinely fasted, but he added that God spoke and told him to stop on day three of his last fast.

The next day I received a book, *The Fasting Prayer*, and when I randomly opened it, the word Daniel leaped up at me. I'd never dieted or fasted in my entire life, but I was immediately inspired to begin my first water-only fast. I managed far better than I expected and made it through an entire workweek. Twenty-one days was looking pretty aggressive, so on the eighth day, I asked God if I could eat again. In the spirit of "you can't make this stuff up," my Apple watch buzzed on my wrist and the random Bible verse of the day popped up: *The body needs physical food, like the soul needs spiritual food.*

Two weeks later, I experienced an unforeseen transition from the difficult role. I am wholeheartedly convinced that God wanted me to be available when COVID broke out, because I soon-after became Vice President of Medical Markets for a company, Hemotek, that had developed powdered oxygen. I raised the money for a university to do testing that proved it worked against COVID. It saved many lives and allowed many others to bypass ventilators. I still serve as a consultant for the company and firmly believe God has greater plans for this product.

In January 2022, I went on my second water-only fast, planning to maintain it for seven days, like before. As I fasted, I asked God for clarity on a certain amount of additional income to support my family, adding it would be even better if the opportunity was spiritually connected. One week later, brilliant fellow veterans Wade Myers and Mark Crumblish hired me on the spot for exactly the dollar amount I'd fasted on, and then Wade led a prayer to end our meeting. Today, the work that Profit Inc. does is exceptionally rewarding, using game-changing financial analytics to increase a company's net profits and business value.

God also appears to me sometimes without a fast. He appeared to me in a vision at 3 a.m. in 2024 when I was driving home from a trip to my daughter's college in Charleston. When I began praying about the vision, I paid attention to how new opportunities fell into place, and I soon became an equity partner in two new companies. This is another testament to my belief that when I'm aligned with God, what happens is God's plan for my life. A person is never too young or old to have the capacity for God.

My favorite definition of *success* is one I learned several years ago at a TIGER 21 National Conference in Beverly Hills (TIGER 21 is a by-invitation-only group for high-worth individuals). The speaker, Adam Gran, author of *Give and Take*, suggested that the world is divided into three categories, the Givers, the Takers, and the Matchers.

Givers give with no expectation that they'll receive anything in return. Takers clearly take, and they don't give back. Matchers will give if they know that they will get something back on a quid pro quo basis. Gran had researched salespeople, medical professionals, and engineers to determine not only which group they fit into, but how traditionally successful they were. He posed the question that I routinely ask others: *Which of these three groups finishes* **last** *in revenues, earnings, and all the usual measurements of success?* Most answers are optimistic and suggest that Takers or Matchers finish last, but it's actually the Givers who finish last.

Therefore, the next question is: *Which group finishes* **first?** The natural answer is either Takers or Matchers, but surprisingly, the Givers also finish first! Eventually what they give comes back to them in sufficient volume to more than compensate their generosity and then catapult them ahead of the other two groups. Givers also add the most value to teams and companies.

When I told my wife, Cherryl, about Gran's analysis, she said, "I *finally* get you!"

Related to giving, I love the philanthropic community and routinely speak to law firms, accounting firms, and networking groups on the value of philanthropic networking, where a person purposely brings time, talents, and resources in order to generate a strong business network. For 10 years, I served as the Philanthropic Consultant for *Philanthropy in Texas* magazine, later *Philanthropy World*, as I traveled with the Founder, Bob Hopkins, to interview the most active philanthropists.

Today, I focus my charitable efforts on my passions: Christian work, supporting veterans, and fighting child sex trafficking.

Though Christian and veterans' causes take a good deal of my time and effort, my greatest philanthropic passion is to fight the evil of domestic child sex trafficking. I could write an entire book on the story of Jaco Booyens, founder of Jaco Booyens Ministries (www.helpjbm.org), and his sister, Ilonka, who was trafficked for six years in the music industry. By God's hand, she is healed and healthy now. My involvement began in 2012 when Jaco asked me for help with a movie he was hoping to make about sex trafficking, 8 Days. It is a true story about eight days in an underaged girl's life, when she was raped by at least 50 men.

Another of the many Forrest Gump-like serendipitous happenings in my life took place just before we began shooting the movie in 2013. I'd gone to a cybersecurity conference with hundreds of attendees. After the first couple of boring presentations, I was ready to leave when a speaker from Homeland Security said from the podium, "I know I'm here to talk about cybersecurity, but what's on my heart is child sex trafficking." I knew at that moment why God had sent me there.

The speaker went on to say the agency had just broken up a trafficking ring in Dallas, rescuing 30 girls and arresting 100 johns. None of us were going to see it on the evening news or read about it in the newspaper because the perpetrators were elected officials, clergy, and business leaders who would never let the story get out. Homeland Security and the FBI could not get their arms around the proliferation of transactions driven by porn sites and the dark web because they can only intervene if they can identify a transaction as underage or a girl missing.

After his talk on cybersecurity, I was waiting for the agent and told him about the movie we were making. He said, "I'm in! If the film will make the public more aware and help train my agents, I want to be a part of the movie."

Jaco's wife, Philipa, rewrote the script to include real Homeland Security agents rescuing our film's star. We were turned away from several motels which didn't want us to film on-site. A motel finally agreed to let us film, and just before shooting the rescue scene, the agents suddenly removed the blanks from their weapons, loaded real ammunition, moved three doors down from the room where we were shooting the rescue scene, and kicked in the door.

They'd just received word that a real trafficking victim, one missing for 16 months, was in that room. They rescued her and arrested the two men who had paid to rape her. The agents then replaced their rounds with blanks, returned to our rented room, and "rescued" our young actress.

> A person is never too young or old to have the capacity for God.

You can't make this stuff up! *8 Days*, released in 2014, is still available for sale or rent on streaming sites such as Amazon Prime.

* * *

My parents, Johnny and Junette Clayborn, are the salt of the earth and the most influential people in my life. For almost two decades, they've been the 24/7 caregivers for my younger sister, Colleen Jessie, who was run over by a drunken driver. I see myself as a blend of both parents, my organized, empathetic, artistic mother, and my disciplined, science-minded, athletic dad. While I was still in junior high, Dad had me place a poster board above my bed with my goals and objectives on it. I wrote them down in black and checked them off with comments in red, and I believe that practice helped me on my journey to West Point.

I met the next most influential person when Cherryl sat down next to me at a bar. She was serving as wingman for a friend who wanted to meet me, "the salt-and-pepper guy." I never noticed the friend, and at 39, I fell in love with the fabulous woman who's been my wife for more than 20 years. A multi-cultural, multi-racial beauty, she was born in Kingston, Jamaica, and moved to the United States as a child. She's fearless, and she has made me a better man—more proactive, less gullible, and (fortunately) much better dressed.

When I was 43, our daughter, Carly, was born. Being father to such a remarkable young woman has been the blessing I didn't know I needed. One of my goals is to take Carly up in space, something we have both dreamed about for years.

My life has been remarkably blessed, I realize. I discovered you can't truly have a meaningful relationship with God unless you've suffered. Without suffering, there is no witness to others. It's hard to ask God to use you if you haven't been used in a way that exhibits God's love. I have also done my best to follow God's lead in forgiving others, regardless of their transgressions against me.

Famously, John 3:16 says, "For God so loved the world that He gave His one and only Son, that whoever believes in Him shall not perish, but have eternal life." Christ paid the ultimate price for our sins by suffering on the cross. Christianity is not about protocols or hierarchy or titles, but about love and grace, which are granted to anyone willing to follow.

Today, I manage several video conferences and meetings daily for the six different companies God has directed me to lead or facilitate, and I always close with a peace sign. Peace is also represented on the front cover photo on this book; my West Point ring is on my left hand, which is making a peace sign, while my right hand is palm up, representing giving to others and receiving from God.

God provides a thread of connectivity, the direction He wants you to go, as well as the will and the plan He has for you.

It's not good enough to be alive—you must be proactively alive. The key is learning to *pay attention.*

# ABOUT CARY CLAYBORN

The first young student-athlete from his rural Arkansas high school to attend the U.S. Military Academy at West Point, Cary Clayborn has led an exciting, Forrest-Gump-type life full of serendipitous events on his way to becoming a successful philanthropist, entrepreneur, and teacher of spiritual lessons.

As a young Army officer at the heart of the Cold War, he learned to work under pressure and with grace and diplomacy. Later, his pre-med degree and master's in business had him teaching advanced techniques to heart surgeons and working as a financial advisor. He's also gained equity in a diversified number of companies, all unique to the market and all based on faith in the support of others.

Veterans' causes consume much of Cary's non-profit and for-profit efforts, and vulnerability of veterans in the health care system is the focus of one company in which he's an owner.

Cary found his calling in fighting domestic child sex trafficking, collaborating on and producing **8 Days**, a film based on a true story that revealed the growing danger to unsuspecting, underaged girls.

His life advanced in 2019 when he first heard the voice of God in a dream, and again in 2020 after a seven-day water-only fast. Since then, he has learned one must go through suffering to reach a place of witness, connectivity, and opportunity, and he knows whatever happens is God's plan for his life.

Cary lives with his wife Cherryl in the Dallas-Fort Worth Metroplex, and his cherished daughter Carly attends college in Charleston. He has a goal of taking Carly on a journey into space, something she has yearned for since she was very young. Another goal is to play golf at 1,000 different courses around the world; he's currently played almost 800 courses in 45 states and 17 countries.

 ovou.com/carygclayborn

 cary-clayborn-196a32

# Create the Life You Desire

NETASHA REED

My adult life began all too abruptly when I was just 13, hardly even a teenager, and I gave birth to a little girl of my own. I dropped out of school at 15 when my second daughter was born, and earned my GED at 18, the same year my first son was born.

By the time I was 21, I had five children, and according to most statisticians, I should be living my life as an impoverished hot mess. Toss into the mix that I am the daughter of two people with substance use disorders, and the odds of my having an accomplished and wealthy life should be laughable.

Now I'm in my early forties. My children are loving, educated adults with fulfilling careers and strong relationships. Some of them have children of their own, and my family is large, caring, and close-knit. I have built many highly successful businesses and continue to create more. I have established a family trust to care for generations of my children and their offspring, and I have a family compound large enough for everyone to build their own home for vacation or even permanent use.

I tell people I manifested my own life. Through my efforts, I've become a multi-millionaire, a bona fide top-producing giant who spends much of my time helping others succeed. Statistics don't begin to define my story.

How can such a reversal of fortunes happen?

No matter what the obstacles are, I manage to do just what the title of this chapter promises: *I work my way past whatever tries to stop me and continue creating the life I desire.*

No, I didn't find a magic wand. My success is an unstoppable force, built on persistence, hard work, and my steadfast refusal to accept *"no"* for an answer. So far, I haven't encountered an immovable object, and I'm determined not to. Ever.

Yes, my childhood ended sooner than it should have. My mother, my two sisters, and I lived in a small house behind my grandparents' big family house. My mother and my grandparents were at the center of my life, and my father was never a part of it at all.

I admire my mother, Darlene; she worked hard in my grandfather's business and instilled in me a strong work ethic and a hustle mentality. She taught me a great deal about being a woman. But she also showed me everything I did not want to be as a mother and a parent. I felt I had something to prove to her and to my father, who didn't claim me until I was older and no longer needed his parenting.

My grandparents had the most significant impact on me because they raised me and provided me with the love and affection I had missed. I honored my grandmother with the name "Mom," and she and Grandpa became the center of my life. Mom taught me how to love unconditionally; she generated peace around her, and she showed people the way to believe in God.

Mom loved me, brought me to church, told me I was smart, if maybe a bit "fast," and she was there for me when I made decisions with which she didn't agree. Even then, she never raised her voice. She gave me a great deal of leeway, which I needed, and always provided her full support.

Mom was Julia Kay Smith, a god-fearing woman and a well-known evangelist in East Chicago, Indiana, and the surrounding area. She made sure we went almost every Sunday to her nondenominational church, growing up in a strongly religious environment, knowing the value of family and what was right or wrong.

Grandpa was the only father I knew, an entrepreneur and a deacon at his Baptist church, which we attended on special occasions. While his business was illegal gambling, a numbers business—which sounds contradictory to his church-going persona—he was still a wonderful, honest, and ethical man. He died when I was in fifth grade, and it was painful.

Mom and Grandpa are the reason I am who I am. They taught me that everything I do should be for the betterment of my family, and I still follow what I learned.

Darlene, my sisters, and I lived in the little house behind my grandparents' big house until I was 13. That year was a turning point, a major shift in my life. I became pregnant, the big house burned down, and Mom, Darlene, my sisters, and I moved to Texas. I know they wanted to separate me from my 18-year-old boyfriend, and this was an easy, well-timed option.

When I was 16, I moved out to be on my own with my two daughters, renting a three-bedroom home by myself. I knew it was time for my children and I to make our own family. Within a couple of years, I moved into another house with the man I loved. He became the father of my last three children and my long-term partner.

As much as I loved my children, I was constitutionally unable to become a stay-at-home mother. Instead, my partner became a stay-at-home dad for the next 22 years, while I studied and learned, worked, and transformed our lives. I didn't want our children to pay for my mistakes, and I wanted them to grow up in a two-parent home with one parent dedicated to their day-to-day routines and needs. They had that, though our family never fit into any traditional model.

From a very young age, I always wanted more, and that focused desire gave me a façade of self-assurance, making me seem older and more confident than I was. While that helped me with everything I did as an adult, nobody knew how sometimes I could become riddled with doubt. There weren't many cracks in my façade, and the ones I had were caused by worrying about my children, especially when others told me the way I chose to raise my kids was crazy.

From the beginning, I worked and studied seven days a week to prove myself and support us all. After earning my GED at 18, I attended college to pursue an associate's degree as a medical assistant, with a focus on oncology, hematology, and chemotherapy.

For ten years, I worked for an oncologist who specialized in brain cancers, and I put in a full, demanding week giving our patients chemotherapy treatments in the office. It was not easy; a registered nurse would usually do the work I did. Every weekend, I pulled 12-hour shifts working in a group home for mentally challenged adults. Thank God I stayed healthy during this working marathon.

But no matter how busy I was, I knew I wanted and needed to own a business. My first venture was a cellphone store, a franchise offshoot of the biggest telecom company at the time. I began as the sole proprietor, but after a year, I took in a partner, to my enduring regret. It turned out that he was involved in litigation, which reflected poorly on me in the eyes of the parent company. They refused to allow me to open in a new location, and the business was forced to close. The unfortunate experience gave me my first lesson on doing proper due diligence and the consequences when it's not done, so the lost time and money weren't completely wasted.

I also developed a distaste for having a business partner, a distaste I've maintained for twenty years. I yielded once when my sisters and I had a brief partnership, but I wasn't surprised when that venture didn't end well either.

My next entrepreneurial experience was opening a clothing boutique independently, completely by myself. I was barely in my twenties, and I had some savings which I poured into my second retail attempt. I quickly learned first-hand how tough the mom-and-pop style of entrepreneurship can be as I struggled to pay the bills, come up with creative marketing, order sufficient (but not too much) inventory, train the staff, and make payroll. (Remember, I was working seven days a week in my other two jobs at the same time). I didn't learn how to handle problems fast enough when they inevitably arrived. I also struggled with the best way to develop a solid training program for the employees.

> "Quitting is the only true failure"

Still, I didn't want to quit—I've always believed that quitting is the only true failure. I wanted to own my business, but eventually I realized there had to be a better way. After a couple of years, I closed the doors, liquidated the inventory, and contemplated what I had learned. I realized *I* was the one who truly needed training.

My entry into multi-level marketing (MLM) brought answers to the shortcomings I had begun to recognize. Regardless of the product or service your MLM company offers, it's ultimately about self-improvement. Once I started seeking mentors and coaches and investing in information, my businesses grew exponentially, not just in size but in profitability.

My only regret is that I didn't do it earlier. For the last twenty years, I've never stopped paying for coaching, and I won't, regardless of how successful I become or the kind of businesses I own. I'm still seeking education and self-improvement. We all should. I have gained great mentors over the years who have guided me, too. Having this type of input into your life is like gaining a "cheat code": You collapse decades of learning the hard way into months, even into days in some cases.

I never fear that I'm wasting my time or money buying a program or working with an expert. When I've paid $25,000 for a coaching program and found it to be a less-than-mediocre rehash of something I've already learned, it's still not a waste because I've learned something from it, even if it's what *not* to do.

When I dropped out of high school at 15, it wasn't because I had a problem with learning; I was a straight-A student and always enjoyed learning. Education should be a life-long enterprise, not something you end the day you graduate. We all have something to learn, regardless of our level of success in life. I still reach out to people who do something better than I do, and especially like those with whom I can relate. I've also bought every bit of media that Zig Ziglar, Les Brown, and Johnny Wimbrey have produced.

Johnny was one of the first mentors I paid attention to and followed. I was doing business with his mother-in-law, and she brought him in for a training session. He offered his mentoring program on compact discs, and I bought the complete set. Johnny's teachings set the foundation for my journey.

Coach Stormy Wellington also had a significant influence on me; we shared similar backgrounds, and I saw aspects of myself in her. She helped me learn to believe in myself more fully, to trust my dreams—and to envision where I was headed.

For years, I've done my best to spread the word about the value of mentoring, and I finally developed my own mentoring program. When I realized the people I was coaching in the financial industry were making a fortune but didn't know how to turn their money into true wealth, I developed the Manifesting Millions Mentorship (MMM). I do two sessions a month on Zoom and meet in person with selected business leaders.

Many of the people who take my program come from deprived backgrounds, and they have no idea what to do with their sudden influx of serious money. They need to learn how to manage their finances, invest wisely, and consider their future. They learn to buy items that appreciate, rather than blowing the whole wad on personal belongings which depreciate and have no long-term value. No matter how much you start with, it's all too easy to spend your money quickly and unwisely and end up with nothing.

I show them there's a *science* to building wealth, and there are certain principles to follow. Over the course of months, I teach them who they must become to build and maintain their wealth.

Not only is MMM a course in financial literacy, but it's also an introduction to the joy of learning for its own sake. Teaching my MMM clients to appreciate the value of mentoring and coaching is an equal part of the process. The concept of coaching and mentoring doesn't come naturally to many people, especially those who are bright and think they have become successful and learned it all on their own. It took me far too long to admit it, so I'm understanding, if firm, about the changes they need to make in their mindset.

I have never stopped owning businesses, which means I always have employees who need training. Soon after I closed my boutique, I founded Jazzy Lady Entertainment, which specializes in marketing, promotions, artist management, and tour management within the hip-hop world. That naturally led to franchises I bought in nightclubs and restaurants, and my nickname: I'm known in the entertainment industry as Jazzy da Mogul.

As soon as MMM was in the works, I made it available at no cost to all the people who work with and for me, as one of my key management principles. Though it wasn't designed with my staff and management in mind, giving employees access to MMM isn't just to make them better employees; it has a long-term goal. I want to train my managers, employees, contractors, and franchise buyers on how to replicate my success. I hope that they, too, will step out and create their futures when they're ready, because it's already clear that they're entrepreneurs at heart.

One of the advantages of becoming a de facto adult at the age of 13 is that I was already an experienced adult and entrepreneur by the time I was 24. I wasn't just getting out of college after years of living on an allowance and using a parent's credit card.

My parenting and management skills may have grown more sophisticated, but my money management skills had not. When I realized I was still thinking about money in a simplistic, basic way, I made a point of learning everything I could about finances, business economics, and metrics, as well as the benefits of leveraging other people's money.

A wise use of leveraging and managing debt opens new doors to growth and profitability. Playing by the rules, claiming all of your profits, and paying taxes on them is a significant part of what makes these opportunities available.

If your income is primarily unreported, as it often is with many entrepreneurs, *particularly* minority business owners, you have limited value as a borrower. Hiding money is a short-sighted and illegal solution to a nonexistent problem. It gives you few options to raise capital or ever sell your business. Entrepreneurs undermine their firms with the flimsy and outdated excuse of avoiding taxes.

Running a business should not be a game of hide-and-seek. Paying my taxes is proof that I'm earning a living and being successful. I own corporations; I want to be legitimate and do business properly. I tell everybody, *Do it right!*

Another key peeve: All too often, people are impressed just by the amount of revenue a business generates. What matters is a business's *profitability ratio*—how much profit the company earns from its revenue. It's a key metric that can indicate whether a business is well-run and if it can secure financing, and a significant factor when you calculate the value of a company. Why would you want to damage your asset by denying its profitability?

A short study of mergers and acquisitions will open your eyes to how a business is valued. You need to have a good profitability ratio for at least a couple of years if you're ever going to sell a company for anything close to what it's worth. You always need an exit strategy, even if you plan to hold on to a business forever, and the ability to sell assets for their actual value should be a key part of your plans. You never know how your needs might change.

As I learned about money, credit, and the financial best practices of various businesses, I also learned something about myself that surprised me. I realized I'm not traditionally entrepreneurial in the mom-and-pop store way, like the one I had with my first business. Instead, I prefer buying franchises.

> " Education should be seen as a life-long learning experience, "

The more I learned, the clearer it became: When you license someone else's business model and brand, the start-up bugs have already been discovered and fixed, you have name recognition, there's a marketing program in hand, good reporting and software systems, and there's excellent training for the staff built in as part of the package you buy. There's no need for you to reinvent the wheel.

Of course, there are excellent franchises and terrible franchises, and most are in between. We all know the stories of imploding business empires that crashed from 10,000 locations to none in just a few years. Who sees Howard Johnson's restaurants anymore? (They were the biggest restaurant chain in the U.S. in the 1960s and 1970s.) What happened to Quiznos Subs, which shrank from 4,700 franchises to 200? In that case, Quiznos was gouging the franchisees in every way, from paper products to food, using them as profit centers rather than business partners. Lawsuits bankrupted everyone.

Due diligence is just as necessary when you buy a franchise as when you pour your life savings into starting a one-off business, and it *should* be done both ways. You need the franchisor to back up your investment with all the necessary resources to succeed, including a solid strategic marketing budget and the ability to keep pace with changes in demand and technology, as well as the capacity to innovate. You also need your fellow franchisees to be solid businesspeople, as they protect the brand you share. What is often overlooked is the need for a secure territory, one that won't be threatened if a new franchise opens nearby.

I'm not sentimental about the businesses I buy; it's not as though my life's desire is to welcome guests to my new restaurant or show off my cooking or barkeeping skills to paying customers. I want the business I own or license to be an excellent and reliable one that generates revenue and profits on a long-term basis, even when technology changes, as it surely will.

It's like buying stock; you don't need to be able to build a car if you buy stock in Ford Motors. You do want the corporate suits who run the business to do a good job and stay on top of the marketplace and the supply chains.

The franchises I bought are not part of the same company, and they're not the same type of business. They are an efficient way to expand my stream of both income and profit. I studied what worked and didn't work, what was frustrating, and what looked scalable. They are in the entertainment and restaurant field, high-dollar chains. I enjoy owning them; they're profitable, fun, and very well-run by my employees. There's no plan to copy or improve on the model, and I will keep them just as-is.

My businesses are not family businesses in the sense that I don't intend to manage their inner workings myself, nor do I expect my children or grandchildren to work in them. That's not how I view generational wealth. These businesses are investments designed to generate an efficient stream of profit, whether I own them outright or collect royalties from my franchisees.

Still, all my businesses matter deeply to me, and I'm very picky about the managers who work with me or do business with me. They must be open to growth and be completely aboveboard. I want them to feel invested in my businesses, as if they are the owners, and treat them and my employees well.

I differ from many owners in that I don't expect to hold onto my managers for very long. It's not that I treat them poorly or work them to death—I treat them very well. I expect they're on the same path that I'm on, and I want to educate them and help them reach that point. When they're ready to start their business ventures, I wish them well.

The next step was natural for me: I began to develop new businesses to franchise and license to others. I knew what works and what doesn't from years of owning and studying them. I know the optimum formula from my franchises; it's a matter of perfecting and simplifying the business so that it can be easily replicated, one that fits different geographic markets, is easy to run (though, of course, nothing is foolproof) and requires a relatively small initial investment. I knew I'd need to create excellent training for the franchisee and their staff.

The businesses I'm beginning to roll out and license to others are very different from the ones I bought.

One's Jazzy Lady Printing, a full-service printing company that also designs and prints custom marketing and promotional products, not just brochures. We pack and ship items for customers, of course. We differ from most other printer/shippers because we don't have mailbox service, and don't plan to. It focuses on printing and creating promotions. The stores are built on a friendly, mom-and-pop-type framework, and they have a welcoming feel. It's an easy-to-run business that doesn't require a large staff to operate efficiently and doesn't necessitate a substantial financial investment.

Maximum Tax Pros and Consultation is very close to my heart. It offers financial services that include tax preparation, tax planning, credit repair, and credit building, catering to both individuals and businesses. We don't provide bookkeeping services. I started the company fifteen years ago and now have four locations of my own.

The company offers our clients classes in credit and taxes; hundreds of people have taken them. We also provide courses for tax preparers and professionals nationwide. We offer packages to tax professionals, including licensing our proprietary tax preparation software, full franchises, and extra options that build the business. We also provide branding and marketing materials, as well as team-building packages.

I am just as proud of Getting to the Profits Online University. When I moved to Georgia in 2019, my daughter suggested that I start teaching others how to build a successful business and start earning money. The year I began doing that, I reached my first million-dollar year in only six months. It made me grasp the wisdom behind the saying, "The more people you help get what they want, the sooner you'll get what you want." I keep the courses affordable to just about anybody; tuition can be paid monthly or yearly.

My six-week class, also titled *Getting to the Profits,* teaches the ABCs of being an entrepreneur. Over the weeks, I explain how to be a smart business owner vs. being just someone who owns a business. My clients learn how to build their businesses properly and how to structure them to make a profit. They know how to maintain their credit rating and always remain fundable. And importantly, how to do it with integrity. I don't ever forget that "I" word, because that's what I look for in coaching, mentoring, and any form of education.

We discuss everything from websites to the types of grants and loans available, from logos to recovering after bankruptcy, rebuilding credit, and the use of social media.

One of my ways of giving back to the community is *Start.Grow. Fund,* a free resource I offer through Facebook a couple of times a month. I include a Zoom link to the events, and I ask experts in different businesses to volunteer their time and teach special segments in their field.

Finally, I took the time to start writing books: *The ABCs of Being an Entrepreneur, Unleash Your Undeniable Impact* (with Les Brown and Dr. Cheryl Wood), and *Small Business Survival Guide.* I'm getting my message to business owners through any available medium, and this book marks the next stage of my outreach efforts.

My life has been remarkably satisfying and happy, so when 2019 became a traumatic year for me, I was somewhat overwhelmed. In December 2018, the hip hop artist I'd been managing for a long time was killed. My long-term romantic partnership ended after 22 years; we had grown apart, and we knew it was time to part ways. Our kids were grown, but I realized they were too dependent on me, and they needed to cut some ties and become more self-sufficient.

> " The person who can solve the most problems makes the most money. "

I was suffering from some anxiety and had the kind of chest palpitations that make you feel life is deluging you with pressure from all angles. My support system seemed to temporarily leave me in the lurch without the level of backup I was used to.

To my surprise, I often found myself procrastinating, unwilling to make the decisions my team needed. That was not at all like me. I realized that, while my businesses were still very profitable, I wasn't reaching the life-changing money level. It was time to shake things up and make a change.

In March 2019, I made a pivot. I pulled up stakes in Texas and moved lock, stock, and barrel to the Atlanta area, where I had never lived before—just me. My businesses run themselves, so my constant presence wasn't necessary. I left everything behind, including family. Call it tough love, for us all, including me.

I needed to do something new. As my daughter suggested, I began teaching business classes and spreading my knowledge with others.

What happened? The following year was my most profitable ever. It was a quantum leap forward. Since then, I have not looked back.

As I look ahead, I often remind myself that adversity comes with the territory. When I encounter that inevitable obstacle, I remind myself *that this is what I asked for.* The thought gives me some perspective, and I realize how true it is. What would life be without challenges?

When I encounter problems, I remind myself, *The person who can solve the most problems makes the most money.*

My mindset is *Everything always works out for me.* I must hold on to that, because I need to experience whatever comes my way. I also know that significant changes are still to come as I continue to rise to the next level of income and profitability. I'm just getting started on the next phase, and I have a long journey ahead of me before I reach fulfillment.

Success is different for everybody, both in their imagination and in reality. Initially, I thought money was the accurate measure of success, and now I know that's not the case. Now I know that success is *freedom,* being free from everyday worries and having the time to spend as I want. At this moment, much of what I wish to include is the freedom of time so I can travel with my children and grandchildren.

Creating my family compound is another measure of my success, a small part of the legacy of wealth, business ownership, and love I'll leave for the generations of my descendants.

My most significant success is that everything I'm building is something of value and integrity, something that will always be there for them. Something they can be proud to claim.

I have created my own life, and it's exactly what I want it to be. All that I wanted to become, I became . . . therefore, I am.

# ABOUT NETASHA REED

A striking dynamo also known as Jazzy Lady, Netasha has owned multiple successful businesses since she was barely of legal age. She began her life earlier than most, having her first child at 13, earning her GED at 18, and buying franchises and launching businesses by the time she was 21.

While she was establishing her business empire in her twenties, she also worked seven days a week, as a registered medical assistant with an oncologist during the week and as a caregiver in a group home on weekends. With her long-time partner, she raised five children, who are now successful adults, many with families of their own.

One of her early businesses was Jazzy Lady Management and Promotions, a hip-hop talent management firm. After a few years, this led her to ownership of several high-end clubs and restaurants. Her business life moved into overdrive when she discovered the value and power of coaching and mentoring. Netasha founded Getting to the Profits Online University to help other entrepreneurs succeed, and created *Manifesting Millions Mentorship*, a program she also offers at no charge to her many employees. She periodically offers a free program on Facebook, *Start.Grow.Fund.*

Netasha has begun to roll out franchises in two of the businesses she founded: Jazzy Lady Print & Media, a full-service printing company, and Maximum Tax Pros & Consulting, a company that preaches financial literacy and the difference between revenue and profit. She preaches the value of keeping business on the books, not under the table, of leveraging other people's money, and the science of building wealth that lasts generations.

Netasha has authored two earlier books: *ABC's of Being an Entrepreneur* and *Unleash Your Undeniable Impact.* She enjoys spending her free time in her family compound in Loganville, Georgia, with many of her children and grandchildren.

 www.netashabreed.com

 Netasha Reed

 @jazzydamogul

# Be Bold!

NDIDI MUSA, M.D.

wrestled with failure and self-doubt for decades, never realizing I was leading a bold and extraordinary life. Today, I am filled with clarity and a sense of fulfillment, close to achieving one of my boldest goals: fostering a culture of coaching in medicine, a place where there has never been one.

It's not a coincidence that I needed help from a coach of my own before I could recognize my worth and potential. As I learned the values and techniques of coaching and became an executive coach, I finally found my full voice. Now, I am ready and able to share this truth with anyone who feels the same lack of courage I felt most of my life: *Nothing is impossible—you can reach your highest potential.* If sharing my journey and my experience inspires you to find your strength and perseverance to believe in what you can do, then I have reached another stepping stone on the path to my own goal.

My parents were brilliant, courageous individuals shaped by history and adversity. In 1959, they moved to London, where my father, Jacob Agwu, took a position with the Nigerian Embassy as a recruitment officer. Though educated as an economist, his diplomatic job was to convince expatriate Nigerians to return to their country as it prepared for independence from Great Britain in 1960. My mother, Europa Wilson-Agwu, left for the United States to obtain her master's degree in education from the University of Colorado. I was born while she completed her degree in the United States. We returned to England when I was six months old. After two years in England, my father was reposted, and he decided to leave diplomatic service and return home to Nigeria, where he joined the newly independent government.

My mother was born in Sierra Leone, a country established for formerly enslaved British people and those caught on the high seas. Great Britain granted Sierra Leone its freedom in 1961. My father was Nigerian, a patriot, and a member of the Igbo ethnic group. The Igbos were the ethnic majority in the southeastern region of Nigeria, later called Biafra. When Biafra seceded from Nigeria in 1967, my family was in the middle of the conflict.

Igbos had been targeted and killed in other regions of the country for years, and a million migrated to Biafra for safety. After the secession, Nigeria declared war and soon blockaded the ports of the newly independent Republic of Biafra. Two million Igbos starved to death before the war ended in 1970 in one of the world's most unrecognized and underreported genocides.

My father quit his job with the Nigerian government and played a pivotal role in Biafra, contributing his logistics expertise to the war effort. He arranged for ammunition and its distribution and used his diplomatic skills to try and get international support. Biafra had a good supply of crude oil but no refineries and the blockade starved us of fuel and food. My creative and talented father played a small part in designing an innovative method to refine oil without a refinery. Meanwhile, my mother worked tirelessly with the Red Cross, transporting refugees to safety in Gabon. My maternal grandmother was visiting from Sierra Leone and stepped in to care for us children.

Our lives changed drastically when we fled Nigeria on a cargo plane; we became refugees overnight and lost everything we had. We eventually migrated to Sierra Leone with my mother and rebuilt our lives. My father remained in what had been Biafra for years, even after the war was lost, because he didn't want to live in another man's country. He always remained a part of our lives, and all of us children spent some time in Nigeria going to school.

In Sierra Leone, I saw the power of education and hard work when my mother became the sole provider for our extended family of seven siblings and cousins, plus household help. Despite the cost, she ensured we all attended private schools, instilling in us the belief that education was the key to success, stability, and a brighter future. She made sure we learned discipline and knowledge and told us we could accomplish anything with hard work.

Our mother was a math teacher and the second Black principal of the Annie Walsh Memorial School, the first girls' school established in sub-Saharan Africa, and a senior traditional math examiner for the West African Exams Council. She also valued much more than just book learning. She opened our eyes to culture wherever we lived and taught us a full life needs more than just academics to be complete. She found time to take us to the plays staged by the British Embassy in Freetown; I remember watching *Julius Caesar*, *Pirates of Penzance*, *The Sound of Music*, and *To Sir, with Love*.

My mother's unwavering strength and commitment to our education, despite adversity, have profoundly shaped my values. Her examples taught me resilience, the importance of sacrifice, and the life-changing impact of hard work and determination. These lessons continue to inspire me in every aspect of my life.

Through education, I've been able to pursue a fulfilling career, make meaningful contributions, and help others navigate their paths to success. Education continues to guide my life, reminding me of my mother's sacrifices and the limitless potential it unlocks.

Most of my siblings are mathematically gifted, even a subvariant of math genius, and I felt overshadowed by them as I grew up. One sister became a mathematician and a Fulbright scholar; two brothers are engineers, and another is an architect. They outshone me at school, and for years I believed I was only average.

During my childhood in Sierra Leone, I was introduced to two people who led me to my life's most important directions. When I was 11 years old, I was fascinated by a movie about a man on the brink of death who was saved when he reached out to Jesus Christ. Dr. Modupe Taylor-Pearce talked with me when I told him about my curiosity, and he introduced me to Christianity. Our discussions led me to the beginning of my full, rich life with Him.

Dr. Priscila Nicole was my childhood doctor and a fantastic role model; she is why I became a physician. She always had time to spend with her patients, showing compassion and kindness. She was a good listener and an excellent communicator, even to a child.

After being raised and attending college in Sierra Leone, I took additional premed studies and attended medical school in Monrovia, Liberia, our next-door West African neighbor. While in school, I had my first mentor and the last one I could have for decades, Dr. Barbara Entsuah. She was a new doctor and a Christian sister who quickly became my dear friend. She encouraged my Christian walk as well as my medical career.

The day I graduated was one of the most meaningful and rewarding moments in my life, when I felt thrilled and fulfilled. It was the culmination of years of hard work, determination, and sacrifice, and marked the realization of a lifelong dream. Standing there, surrounded by family and peers, I felt an overwhelming sense of pride and gratitude—not just for achieving my goal but for the support and encouragement that had carried me through the journey. That moment symbolized personal success and the hope and purpose that drove me to pursue a career dedicated to helping others.

I had waited to marry until I finished medical school. David Musa, a man who loves God as deeply as I do, dated me for years as we studied and planned our new life together. After our wedding, we immigrated to the United States to finish our studies and start our family. We wanted to raise our children away from the civil wars and terror that were taking over our part of Africa. In medical school, I had seen the chaos and instability that led to the beginning of the first civil war in Liberia and remembered my childhood in war-torn Biafra. I was not going to subject our children to that horror. I wanted to see them grow up to be capable adults who were not scarred and traumatized by wars and violence.

> " Don't look at coaching as a punishment but as an investment. "

When David and I moved to the United States, our move was relatively easy because I was a citizen, having been born here, and I obtained a green card for David. He worked and supported us through the next steps in my certification and further education. I'm bemused when I remember how David's career slowly evolved from science to theology. Now, he's a retired adjunct professor of Systematic Theology from the northwest campus of Fuller Theological Seminary.

We raised our three children together as we moved from one academic and medical setting to another. Ndiloma, Ukejeh, and Ngozi were raised in a happier, more stable, and far less dangerous situation than I had, as we hoped. Our family always ends our conversations with "I love you," which I'd started to do with my late father well before he died. I continue to do that with my long-lived mother, who lives with me and is 98 years old as I write this. Her sister lived to be 102, so I have hopes of her exceeding that.

Coming to America was a shock—but not a cultural change, because I always observed what was happening, read widely, and even watched some low-brow American television. What shocked me was the U.S. educational system. I had to pass the Educational Commission for Foreign Medical Graduates (ECFMG) exam, a test designed for foreign-trained doctors, before I could do post-graduate medicine and practice medicine in the United States. I stayed home with my first child while preparing for the exam, and David studied at Wheaton College and worked to support us.

I was confident I knew the material I was to be tested on, though I had to review the basic science I'd studied in my first two years of medical school for the initial test section. But the testing itself! I had never seen a test like the one I needed to take. Like others raised in the British academic system, I had never been tested with anything but essay questions. This was perhaps the most important test of my life, but for the first time I was facing multiple-choice questions and answers. I asked myself, *How am I supposed to show the examiner the depth of my knowledge by choosing one of these incomplete answers? I know the material so well!* But then I failed the test, an unimaginable shock to my confidence.

This was a pivotal moment for my career, and I quietly thank the Lord I wasn't too stubborn and rigid to recognize it. I needed to put my ego aside, forget how well I'd have done on an essay test, and take a deep breath. I was willing to accept that taking a multiple-choice test must be more complicated than I'd imagined, and finally understood answering the questions was an art. Now it was time for me to learn the technique. I would need coaching.

David and I borrowed money so I could take the best prep course available, and when I took the test again, I passed easily. I was now able to practice medicine in the U.S.

By asking for coaching, I learned more than just how to pass a test. This was the beginning of my journey of self-improvement, the genesis of my efforts to adapt and become more resilient. From that moment, I began to appreciate flexibility and realize it was a vital aspect of my personality.

My residency in pediatrics was at the University of Chicago. My studies and practice went smoothly, especially when I met Dr. Madelyn Kahana during my fellowship in Pediatric Critical Care. I look back on our time together with special appreciation because she taught me to ask the question, "Why?" However, work was generally lonely in Chicago, and I felt overlooked. Of course, I never stepped up and showed my light; instead, I kept it under the proverbial bushel basket.

I realized I was the sole Black woman in a sea of white faces when I took my first job out of fellowship and moved to Indiana University-Purdue University Indianapolis (IUPUI). There was nobody who looked like me to help me along the way, and I was lonely there as well. But I was in the vanguard of the Pediatric ICU, so I dove in and was undeterred. Dr. Mopelola Akintorin, a dear friend whom I met in Chicago during my residency days, became a source of encouragement to me. We prayed together regularly, and she sent me scripture references that helped me rely on my faith.

Next, I left Riley Children's Hospital and went to Cincinnati Children's Hospital, where I did a one-year fellowship in Pediatric Cardiac Critical Care. I then moved to the Medical College of Wisconsin, where I helped build the Pediatric Cardiac Critical Care Program in Milwaukee.

Then, I completed a clinical scholar's program to develop my research skill set. A major organization rejected the first grant I applied for. (I was told I was "too junior" to apply for this meritorious scholarship.) Instead, a grant from the Department of Pediatrics at the University of Washington fortuitously led me to a career in global health, where I became a pioneer.

In most of Africa, an intensivist, or ICU specialist, who works with extremely sick patients, is not recognized as a specialist. I trained and mentored three intensivists in critical care and ER in Ethiopia and began looking for ways to improve training and help more. Next, I mentored physicians who became intensivists in Ghana and continued looking for ways to improve training and lower the extremely high infant mortality rate that has affected so much of Africa.

Medicine has advanced enormously in the last few decades, and we quickly forget how primitive it was until recently. Triage wasn't used until the 1980s, except in military hospitals in war zones. ICU units didn't exist until the 1950s, and cardiac critical care units began to be used in the 1960s. The poorer countries were decades behind the advanced world, and I wanted to do everything I could to help them catch up.

I'd been told I was becoming too pointed in my criticisms. In many ways, that had been the pattern throughout my career. I could speak up confidently for my patients and for my projects, but rarely with the same clarity or courage on my own behalf. For a moment, I wondered if I should simply be quieter, take up less space. But somewhere beneath that doubt, I knew the real issue wasn't the volume of my voice.

The University of Washington offered me carte blanche for my global health work in Africa, so we moved to Seattle in 2013, where David was also welcomed as an adjunct professor. I arrived as a senior attending physician, a pediatric cardiac intensivist, and an associate professor. While the university welcomed me warmly, I was surprised to learn that my style was seen as quite direct—sometimes too critical. Recognizing this, the university offered to support my growth by arranging a coach at their expense.

At first, offering a coach seemed unfair. Before 2020, coaching was considered only a punitive step in the medical field. I was mortified and resentful. Then, a wise friend, Dr. Emeric Palmer, told me a life-changing phrase, and I'm grateful I listened: *Don't look at coaching as punishment but as an investment.* The words triggered a switch inside me, and my attitude changed.

A few years later, I hired my own coach, Paul Martinelli, and continued to evolve. My coach and I focused on what I wanted to be able to do to achieve my potential. The way I approached people improved; I became more self-aware. My communication style evolved—it became more diplomatic, yet it came from a place of self-confidence. My life was enriched.

The pandemic was a pivotal moment, opening my eyes to the critical importance of adaptability. As the world shifted beneath medicine's feet and uncertainties loomed, I came to the stark realization that I was unprepared for the next chapter of my life beyond medicine. I was forced to pause and reflect on my path and purpose.

> " Helping and supporting young doctors as they transition from learning to doing so may forever change their outlook on their careers. "

The period of introspection helped me uncover my "why"—the driving force behind my desire to empower others and make a meaningful impact. That journey of self-discovery ultimately led me to become an executive coach. I thought, *What a great opportunity to learn the art of coaching and coach others to focus on their passions and dreams, to navigate their challenges and find clarity, to recognize they have what it takes to accomplish them, no matter what others say.* I realized I could share, "What voice will you listen to? The one saying you can do it, or the one saying you cannot? Move past your limiting beliefs."

Those negative voices had spoken to me for years, and my limiting beliefs had blocked me, so I was coaching from first-hand experience.

Before the pandemic, I was constantly on the go, practicing global health, with no time to think about my next steps. When the pandemic began, I realized I did not know *what I would do.* I joined the John Maxwell team because I was curious and reached out; what I read about his leadership development resonated with me. It was amazing—all of these people were investing in their personal growth, while I'd just been investing in my professional growth for decades. That was the missing link for me, and I recognized the great opportunity to shift from a fixed mindset to a growth mindset.

Let me give you an example of my mindset: My daughter, a Harvard graduate, quit her first job less than a year after she was hired. I was horrified and said firmly, "We're African! We don't quit jobs. You find a way to rise above what bothers you and find a way to make it work." That's what *I* had done all my life, kept my nose to the grindstone, ignored the voices telling me to leave or change my attitude, and kept a rigid mindset.

Success had eluded me, as I was so narrowly focused on the grindstone, no matter what prestigious awards I'd gathered. I'd been on the World Federation of Pediatric Intensive Care board and been a fellow in the College of Critical Care Medicine, and I was ripe for advancement. Still, I had not risen to my level of success. I regret I unknowingly held my fixed mindset for much of my career. My limited perspective shaped how I approached challenges and opportunities. I didn't realize how this fixed mindset was holding me back from growth, fulfillment, and the ability to see the bigger picture.

Everything began to improve once I recognized the importance of adopting a growth mindset and investing in my life outside of medicine. By embracing new experiences, exploring other interests, and consciously broadening my focus, I discovered new opportunities for personal and professional growth. Not only did I add better balance to my life, but I also began to thrive in ways I hadn't imagined.

Soon, I became certified as an executive coach through the Hudson Institute of Coaching program, and I started a program for the University of Washington Department of Pediatrics, "a developmental coaching program for early career faculty." I thought it was especially important to help early-career doctors, those transitioning from fellowships or residencies to attending physicians, go from training to becoming full-fledged decision-makers in one fell swoop. It's a difficult and frankly terrifying transition at times, and traditionally, it's done without minimal support.

I hope to change this.

Medicine is in crisis, though not enough people recognize this yet. Helping and supporting young doctors as they transition from learning to doing so may forever change how they see their careers. My career would have been far better if I'd had help at that critical time.

When an opportunity arose right in front of me, I took advantage of it, and I applied to become interim chair for my section of pediatric cardiac critical care. I never would have applied for the position if a coach hadn't helped me see my potential and change my lifelong mindset. As part of my application, I wrote out my accomplishments, and I was pleasantly shocked. For the first time, I recognized how much I'd done. I had never before given myself credit.

I was appointed co-chair and decided to focus on impact rather than the title, so I dove in. Leadership is influence, and I planned to make the most of the position and opportunities I finally could grasp.

I had a revelation that I needed to celebrate my colleagues, so I implemented certain practices that help us celebrate each other.

As a first step, I asked everyone to spend 15 minutes telling the rest of us what they do outside of clinical medicine. It opened my eyes, and the eyes of others, to our group's impressive depth and wealth of experience and knowledge. Then, I started the CICU Celebration; our colleagues in the Cardiac Intensive Care Unit inspire each other as we share challenges and unifying events. Every time we meet, I ask, *What can we celebrate? Who can we celebrate today?*

The response from my colleagues has been fantastic.

Next, when we huddle before our CICU rounds, I call the names of two nurses and health professionals who have done something worthy of recognition and express gratitude to them. Our culture began to change with just these few changes over time.

Like my colleagues, I have a rich life outside of my work. My three children are grown and have great careers at three different corners of the North American continent. As I hoped, they have become thoughtful, good adults whom David and I are very proud of.

Since my introduction to Christianity when I was eleven, I have loved sharing the love of Jesus with others. It brings me immense joy and fulfillment to connect with people, offer encouragement, and show kindness in ways that reflect my faith. David and I share our Christian beliefs, and it has been a comfort and part of the underlying structure of our long and happy marriage.

I also love cooking and entertaining others, which brings people together and creates a sense of community. Preparing and sharing food has deep meaning in all African countries; sharing meals and laughter around a table fosters connection and joy, reminding me of the importance of nurturing relationships.

Traveling, both for work and for pleasure, has deeply influenced me. Exploring new cultures, meeting people from different backgrounds, and experiencing the world's beauty has broadened my perspective, enriched my life, and deepened my appreciation for diversity and connection. I traveled to the Paris Olympics in 2024, and it was a wonderful and entertaining experience.

At this point in my career, the definition of success has evolved from accolades or achievements to relationships. Granted, money is essential, and I like to spend quite a lot of it, but I don't focus on money. I focus on making an impact on people. I learned from John Maxwell to move from success to significance; I soon realized that any definition, including success, needs to include the journey, not the destination.

I am grateful for all the fellows I trained in the United States who make a huge difference there and in sub-Saharan Africa, the programs

I helped start, and the intensivists I taught myself. I feel successful.

When I was younger, my definition of success aligned more with external markers: academic excellence, professional accomplishments, and financial stability. Growing up in a culture where education and hard work were seen as *the* foundation for success, my definition was more limited than it is now.

Over time, my perspective has evolved. Life's challenges, including experiences of loss, resilience, and personal reflection, have taught me that success is more holistic. It's about balance—between career and personal life and between ambition and contentment. Success means living authentically, having the courage to pursue what truly matters, and contributing to the well-being of others.

> "The pandemic was a pivotal moment, opening my eyes to the critical importance of adaptability."

My definition of success now includes living a life of purpose, fulfillment, and impact. It's not solely defined by achievements or accolades but by the relationships I've built, the lives I've touched, and the personal growth I've experienced.

Ultimately, success is a journey, not a destination. It's about striving for excellence while maintaining integrity, prioritizing relationships, and finding joy in the milestones and the moments in between. My journey has shown me that true success lies in living a life aligned with my values and making a difference in the lives of others.

The legacy I hope to leave behind is one of being a Christian who spreads the love of Jesus through my compassion, impact, and empowerment. I want to be remembered as someone who dedicated her life to improving the well-being of others, whether through my work in pediatric cardiac intensive care, my contributions to global health, or my commitment to mentoring and coaching others to reach their fullest potential.

I hope to leave a legacy of leadership that inspires others to strive for excellence while remaining grounded in humility and service. Through my coaching, I want to empower individuals to find clarity, purpose, and resilience, enabling them to create positive changes in their lives and the lives of others.

In Sub-Saharan Africa and beyond, I aspire to make a lasting impact on healthcare systems by training future intensivists and reducing childhood mortality in resource-limited settings. I want my efforts to demonstrate the importance of investing in education, mentorship, and the next generation of leaders. Becoming a Pediatric Cardiac Intensivist reflects years of dedication, perseverance, and an unwavering commitment to improving patient outcomes—not only in the United States but also in resource-limited settings.

It has been gratifying to witness the ripple effect of my efforts in Sub-Saharan Africa, where individuals I have mentored and trained are now developing new Intensivists and making a meaningful impact on reducing childhood mortality. Seeing their work multiply and transform healthcare in these regions is one of the most fulfilling aspects of my career.

Establishing coaching programs and helping physicians navigate their careers is another achievement that I hold dear. Supporting others in overcoming challenges, finding clarity, and thriving personally and professionally is immensely rewarding because it creates a ripple effect, positively impacting patients, families, and healthcare teams. My reach is where I work and where I can help the most.

Ultimately, I want my legacy to reflect a Christian life lived with integrity, love, and dedication—a life that proves the power of perseverance, the value of uplifting others, and the belief that even small actions can create profound and lasting change.

# ABOUT NDIDI MUSA, M.D.

Born in the United States and raised in Boulder, Colorado, London, Nigeria, the short-lived Republic of Biafra, and Sierra Leone, Dr. Ndidi Musa survived a war and became a refugee when she was eight years old.

Her parents, a mathematician/educator and an economist/wartime logistics expert, raised her to be exceptional, though for years, she thought she was the most ordinary of her siblings. After attending school in Sierra Leone, she attended college and medical school in Liberia. She then returned to the United States with her new husband, David, and they chose to raise their family and finish their post-graduate education far from the civil wars decimating Africa.

Dr. Musa became a world-renowned pioneer in global pediatric critical care, focusing on the often-overlooked sub-Saharan region, and trained many doctors in the new medical specialty of critical care, especially as pediatric and cardiac intensivists.

Her post-doctoral fellowships and career took her to the University of Chicago and several of the top teaching hospitals in the United States. She and her family eventually settled in Seattle, where she is a professor of pediatrics at the University of Washington.

Dr. Musa, having experienced discrimination as both a woman and a Black American, recognized that doctors needed mentors, coaches, and sponsors. She became a certified executive and leadership coach. She began and directs the **Internal Coaching Program** at the University of Washington Department of Pediatrics, helping young doctors navigate the transition from residencies and fellowships and providing support to established doctors.

She, her husband, Dr. David Musa, and her mother, Europa Agwu, live in Seattle, and she finds time to travel, cook, and practice her deep Christian faith. Her adult children, Ndiloma, Ukejeh, and Ngozi, live and work in the United States.

 Ndidi Musa

# Bloom Where You're Planted

## COLONEL TAMMY S. HINSKTON, USAF, (RETIRED)

"**Y**ou're never going to be an officer! You'll never make it through this program!" my training instructor screamed at me in front of my fellow officer candidates. It was a horrific first day in the program, and I called my dad that evening, trying to hide my tears from the other cadets.

"I want to give up and come home," I said when I reached him.

My dad, an Air Force lieutenant colonel who'd survived field training decades before, broke through my internal pity party. I listened intently to his pep talk as he reminded me I'm a strong, independent, educated woman who grew up in the military and could succeed in anything I set my mind to.

He also reminded me to remember why I was there and that it wasn't supposed to be easy.

"Take it one hour, one meal, and then one day at a time, and do your best, always," Dad said.

I was ready to change the world when I got off the phone.

My identity has been in the military since my birth at an Air Force Base. I was raised believing everybody knew how to iron their clothes, make beds with hospital corners, and always respect authority. My parents taught me work ethic, how to recover from mistakes, and how *not* to quit. I owe much of my personal and professional success to the lessons they instilled in me as a child.

When I was young, I planned to marry someone in the military and be the ideal officer's wife, just like my mom. I realized early enough that I'd never survive in that role, but I was well into my twenties before I knew I was much more suited to being an officer myself.

We had the typically peripatetic Air Force life—Germany, England, Virginia, Ohio, New Mexico, and back to Germany. In fact, I started kindergarten and finished high school at Ramstein AB, which serves as headquarters for the Air Force in Europe and Africa and the NATO Allied Air Command.

My childhood went smoothly, and I excelled at art, math, and volleyball. But after high school, I couldn't figure out my future. I dropped out of the University of New Mexico during my sophomore year, returned to Ramstein, where my parents remained posted, and worked in catering at the officers' club. It was a harbinger of my future Air Force career, though I never had to come home smelling like food when I was running base clubs and services as an officer.

When my younger sister went off to college at Colorado State University, our father's alma mater, I gave college another try and joined her. I still was drifting, career-wise; my major changed from mathematics (too hard), architecture (too many years to get a degree), and interior design (I couldn't abide the free spirits of my fellow design students), to Human Development and Family Studies, with the intent of getting certified as a teacher. I finally interned and taught living, breathing students during my senior year. I soon realized teaching was not the path for me either!

In the middle of my career crisis, I aged out of the military-dependent identification card or ID program, which took away my access to military bases and the military identity I'd known all my life.

The solution finally hit me, and I signed up for Officer Training School (OTS). Shortly after graduating from college, I received my acceptance. Unfortunately, I had to postpone attending for months after I was concussed during a softball game. The day finally arrived, one I will never forget: November 27, the start of an incredible Air Force career.

After my first-day jitters and my dad's pep talk, I did exceptionally well at OTS and graduated in the top four of my class as Officer Trainee Colonel Hinskton, Mission Support Group Commander. I held on to those eagles as motivation to someday outrank my dad, who'd retired as a lieutenant Colonel. He and my fiancé, EJ, participated in my 1996 commissioning ceremony. My dad shaved his beard, wore his dress uniform, swore me in, and received my first salute. EJ, a technical sergeant in the Colorado Air National Guard, gave me my first salute from an enlisted man, and I gave him the traditional silver dollar in return.

While my career goals included eventually becoming a full colonel and outranking my dad, my leadership style was never focused on self-promotion. My drive to succeed was tempered by my empathy, and I always took care of those I commanded. As I was tested by each new assignment and challenge, my passion to serve my enlisted airmen, officers, and civilian employees never wavered, and I added new leadership and management tools at every posting.

I had the privilege of traveling the world with my family and continuing my education. I was exposed to both excellent and bad leaders, learning from both to become the leader who would wear those coveted eagles, accomplish missions, and impact lives along the way. I learned the valuable tools to lead people with excellence from the shoulders of giants. I have always valued integrity and honor.

EJ and I married four days before I reported to my first posting. I took his last name, perhaps the only traditional part of our marriage. He quit his weekday job and weekend warrior position in the Air National Guard to follow me to my new assignment. He also gave me three bonus babies when we married—not exactly babies, but his two beautiful girls, Jaime and Brandy, and a teenage son, Jeremy. Our children spent holidays and summers with us as they grew up, and we are a close family.

The South was a shock to me. EJ, my husband, is Black, and we were not prepared for overt racism, as we realized when he was profiled by a security guard at my OTS graduation in Alabama. It turned out that Arkansas' racism was just about as loud and proud as it was in the deep South. I met a realtor when I was house-hunting off-base on my own. The realtor reassured me, a blonde officer, "This is a safe neighborhood and a great place to live because there are only two Black families."

"We're *done* looking," I snapped, and quickly returned to my car. Later, I discovered I could have reported her, and she would have lost the right to work with military families. I wish I'd known.

Since EJ paid child support, and I was paying off student loans, we weren't in a position to live solely on my second lieutenant's salary. While he waited for a full-time Air National Guard position to open up, he took whatever work he could find, which turned out to be dragging ball fields. Unfortunately, he was a big-city guy from Denver who didn't like anything resembling outdoor wildlife. He hated the bugs, dust, and humidity and despised coming home dirty every night. He stuck it out and finally landed a full-time position on base as a Technical Sergeant. Unfortunately he had to find a new job every time we relocated over the course of my career.

As a young officer, I worked hard to develop my leadership skills and take care of my people. I started as a food service officer, afraid I would fail because I wasn't a great cook. My dad reminded me I was there to lead and not to cook, a lucky thing for everyone who ate at the dining hall. I learned to ask many questions and also to trust but verify. I started to hit my stride when I standardized operations across three facilities. I made sure I knew fully what our needs and shortfalls were so that when a senior leader stopped by, I could give my elevator speech requesting funds. It worked; I landed $65,000 for facility maintenance and repairs; my boss was flabbergasted.

My parents had taught me to "bloom where you're planted" because you don't know who is watching or where this job will lead. That lesson has always influenced my career—no place more strongly than in Little Rock. Arkansas was the last place I wanted to go, but I worked hard, cared for my people, volunteered to repair homes after tornados hit the surrounding towns, and helped build houses with Habitat for Humanity. When the resource management position became unexpectedly vacant, I was selected to fill it and run the flight. I was a second lieutenant, filling the position of a GS-12, which is equivalent to a major. I was picked because I could lead, not because of my accounting skills.

> " My career was my responsibility. "

I bloomed, and most people on base knew me because of my accomplishments at such a junior grade. Because I had bloomed, I was selected as a full-time student for a coveted position to attend the University of Las Vegas, Nevada. I obtained my Master of Science in Hotel and Restaurant Administration, which set me up for a successful career in the Air Force.

Unfortunately, not everything at my first post was perfect. My bosses discovered my husband, the highly visible and popular DJ at the officers' club, was an enlisted member and tried to bring us up on bogus fraternization charges. The creation of fraternization rules was meant to keep the chain of command untainted, with no romantic relationship allowed between an officer and an enlisted service member in their command structure. In our case, we were in different chains of command with absolutely no overlap; we had dated for three years before I even thought of a career in the Air Force. EJ and I were extra careful about being seen together on base in uniform, though it was fun having him salute me in public!

My Commander changed close to the end of my time at Little Rock AFB. The new Commander treated me like dirt and accused me of things I hadn't done. However, he didn't realize I had a reputation as an outstanding officer with the wing commander. I went over his head and made a formal complaint about his toxic, discriminatory, and unprofessional behavior. The Commander was counseled for his behavior, and I was super happy to get orders and leave that toxic environment.

We wanted to have a child as soon as possible, but my first pregnancy ended with a heartbreaking miscarriage. Our daughter, Toni, finally arrived shortly after my promotion to First Lieutenant; it was one of the happiest moments in my life. She's now 26 with her first child, and I wish her the same happiness that she always brought EJ and me.

I left Little Rock with the well-grounded understanding that it was up to me to bloom where the Air Force planted me; my career and happiness were my responsibilities. I won multiple awards at Little Rock, but didn't make my boss write them. Instead, I wrote them and submitted them after trusted peers edited them. Bosses are busy. They are happy to submit awards when deserved, but writing award packages takes time. Taking the initiative to give them a starting point increases the chances of submission.

I've operated on two beliefs throughout my career: *(1) Do not leave your career in someone else's hands, and (2) bloom where you're planted.*

The Air Force values education, and this was just the first of 15 separate educational opportunities I was afforded during my service. I was promoted to captain while I was still in school, and after I received my master's degree I was assigned to Nellis AFB just north of Las Vegas. EJ earned a traditional billet with the Reno Air National Guard and became a resident DJ at Caesar's Palace. After the extreme humidity in Arkansas, we appreciated Nevada and its climate, and neither of us were ready to leave Las Vegas yet.

My first deployment was to Aviano AB, Italy, to run the contingency complex in 2001. Two weeks after my arrival, we watched the September 11 attacks on TV. It was an uncertain few hours while we figured out what was happening and took action to secure the contingency complex. Here, I learned I excelled as a leader in a high-stress, unpredictable, and often dangerous environment. I returned to my Combat Support Flight Commander position at Nellis AFB for only a few months when I was deployed again to an undisclosed location. For six months, a female captain and I lived in a large tent with eight men on the other side of a six-foot interior wall.

Deployments often created a leadership challenge for me, particularly in countries where men don't do business with women. When I negotiated contracts, I was always accompanied by my male contract specialist, to whom the local power broker spoke, though the contract specialist always reminded the local leader that I was the decision maker. I treated my opposites respectfully, understood their culture, and hoped they'd reciprocate someday. Just before I left, the decision-maker finally spoke directly to me; I took it as a diplomatic win.

Following my Nellis AFB assignment, I spent the next three years in planning at the Air Expeditionary Force Center at Langley AFB. EJ retired from the Guard to follow me to Virginia and supply full-time parenting to Toni during our transitions before looking for a job for himself. Soon after my promotion to Major, I was assigned for two years to RAF Mildenhall, England, as the Services Squadron Commander, overseeing a team of 456 military and civilian personnel. I was responsible for a $14.7 million budget and ran 29 businesses and activities across 71 facilities.

Mildenhall was where my leadership moved to the next level. I more actively mentored young enlisted members as they were adjusting to the military life, especially young women who were often struggling so far from family. I helped them gain self-confidence and learn their value.

While in England, I polished my diplomatic and advanced leadership skills, a valid prerequisite for my future work at the Pentagon. I usually watched my words closely, except in one staff meeting when my brain broke and I accidentally called the Wing Commander "honey" during a discussion of post-Thanksgiving football at the Officers' Club. I was mortified, but everyone else, especially the Wing Commander, found it hilarious. When I tried apologizing, he said, "Don't! It was the best time I ever had at a staff meeting my entire career." I didn't live down "honey" for weeks. I learned that as a leader, you can't take yourself too seriously; it's good to laugh at your mistakes.

A third deployment to the United Arab Emirates took six months from the middle of my Mildenhall assignment. I was shocked when my eight-year-old daughter asked me if I had ever deployed before; she didn't remember that I had missed her third and fourth birthdays. This time, I pre-purchased and wrapped gifts for all the holidays/events I'd be absent from and filled a jar with one piece of candy for every day I'd be gone so she'd have a visual reminder of when I'd be home. I read books on DVD so she could watch me read to her. It was essential to stay connected to my family while I was gone. Video chatting wasn't available yet, just email and two 15-minute phone calls a week.

From England, we spent a year at the Naval Command and Staff College, where I earned my second master's. Then, Washington, D.C., became our stable home for the next nine years. My first Pentagon posting was three years as a Protocol Officer in the Office of the Chairman of the Joint Chiefs of Staff, during which time I was promoted to Lieutenant Colonel.

Here, I learned humility. I had come from positions where I had a large amount of both power and responsibility, but in protocol, I represented the CJCS. No one in the office was allowed to send anything out unless it had been checked by someone else to ensure it was error-free. I never realized how many mistakes I made; my goal was to get my products through error-free. I learned to welcome others' input and corrections because they made me better.

I moved into Public Affairs for the Secretary of the Air Force as Chief of Integrated Plans and Strategy. After the first year, I won the Action Officer of the Year Award and spent the second year deployed.

From 2013-14, I deployed to shut down the Transit Center at Manas in the Kyrgyz Republic, which had been a transfer point since 2001 for soldiers headed to Operation Enduring Freedom in Afghanistan. When I left for my year away from my family, Toni was 14, and it was not the easiest time to have your mother deploy. She and I have always been close, and I called her "my mini-me." When I don't recall something that happened while she was in high school, Toni reminds me plaintively, "That's the year you *left* me."

Four months before we closed the Transit Center, the base store ran out of sanitary products for women, which was unacceptable. I made phone calls to get resupply, calling up to the highest levels, but the store's leadership didn't want to get stuck with excess supply since we were shutting down. I finally gave up, went to the base chaplain, and asked him to contact his chaplain friends back in the United States to send us sanitary supplies. The chaplains came through, and we received many large boxes of supplies; we set them out in the women's dorm to take as needed, completely free. About a month later, the store on base finally received sanitary products. I've always believed there's more than one way to skin a cat. If regular channels didn't value our women, I'd find someone who did.

When I returned to the Pentagon, I became Senior Military Advisor to the Deputy Assistant Secretary of Defense for Military Community and Family Policy. I was back working with military members and their families, which was my passion. While in this position, my ability to lead a diverse group of people grew along with my ability to bloom where I'm planted. I trusted God to send me where He wanted me to be since He's bigger than the Air Force, and it was my job to do my very best wherever that ended up being.

Two years later, she was temporarily appointed as the executive to the Assistant Secretary of Defense for Manpower and Reserve Affairs. After 24 hours working for the ASD, he claimed me as his Senior Air Executive Officer, which is where I ended up for the next two years. When promotions came up, he had one "Definitely Promote" to give, and he gave it to me based on my records, history of exceptional performance, and what he'd experienced daily with my leadership. Two men I was competing against for the promotion to colonel told the ASD he was wrong and that they should have received the DP instead of me. One said if he was at "base level," he'd be able to hang out at the bar with the decision-makers and would have gotten the DP. That is the reality of a male-dominated career field, men can hang out with higher ranking male leaders at the bar or on the golf course whereas a female would be looked down upon if she were to hang out with her male peers or bosses at the bar or on the golf course.

Before my promotion ceremony to colonel, my retired dad shaved his beard to read me the oath of office. After the oath was complete, he saluted me and called me ma'am as his voice cracked; there was not a dry eye in the auditorium. When he turned smartly to return to his seat, the soles of his old military shoes disintegrated in a cloud of powdered rubber. Everybody howled, including my family.

While I was in that position, we had monthly birthday celebrations. I was the only woman in the office and a senior officer; however, I was always responsible for cutting and passing the cake and cleaning up after the celebration. After pulling cake duty a few times, I told my co-workers that everyone would be assigned a month to cut, pass, and clean up after the monthly celebration. There was unanimous agreement; everyone understood the unfairness. They honestly hadn't realized they were doing it.

A couple of months later, a new U.S. President was elected, and the ASD was temporarily replaced by a career civil servant, an amazingly talented female leader. During the next monthly birthday celebration, she picked up the knife, cut the cake, and handed the plates to me so I could pass them around. All the men in the office did a masterful job hiding their snickers as I gave them the evil eye. While our acting ASD was a talented servant leader, she managed to undo all I had done to forge equality in our office and ensure women weren't tagged with traditional women's work.

> **Do not leave your career in someone else's hands.**

I finally returned overseas to Ramstein AB; not much had changed since I graduated high school. I served as the Division Chief, Readiness and Integration, for USAFE-AFAFRICA. We were excited to be back and explore Europe together. Toni was able to join us during summer and winter breaks from Denver University.

After two years in Germany, I was assigned another one-year unaccompanied assignment. I served as the 65 Air Base Group Commander of the United States portion of Lajes Field, Azores, Portugal plus Morón Air Base, Spain, two separate installations with runways totaling 130 million square feet. I led 1,200 personnel (military and civilian–U.S., Portuguese, and Spanish), $54 billion in contracts, and 1,200 facilities.

The United States had leased our side of Lajes Field, a Portuguese Air Force base and commercial airport, for more than 80 years since the last half of World War II. The strategic location also led to many rescues, and thanks to its long runways and Atlantic location, it was an alternate landing site for our moon shuttles.

I received three rare honors there, which still give me great pride. The Portuguese Air Force awarded me their Commendation

Medal, which is rarely given to non-Portuguese military officers. My fellow Group Commanders engraved a C-130 cargo aircraft window and presented it to me. The award was a real surprise because only commanders who work on the flight line usually receive them.

My final and most meaningful experience was being promoted to Honorary Chief Master Sergeant. This promotion is rarely given to officers, and it was awarded to me in recognition of how I care for my enlisted troops. Ironically, EJ had given up promotion to Chief Master Sergeant to follow me to Virginia 18 years before. This award is as much his as mine, not just for that reason but because he was always my sounding board and gave me a different perspective. Without his unwavering support, I would not have been as successful as I was.

I had always believed in going to bat for my troops and earned recognition through awards and commendations. I made the most of my craft skills in the Azores, which didn't have the resources other duty posts had. I used my Cricut to make stencils and etch various glass items I could find at the local shops, creating awards and trophies in a pinch. The troops loved them.

For my final two years, I returned to the USAF Headquarters at the Pentagon serving as the Services Operations Division Chief, Manpower, Personnel and Services Directorate, responsible for Services Operations worldwide.

Prejudice against women is sometimes so subtle and ingrained that people have no idea they're doing it, even in this modern age. My birthday cake and sanitary supplies stories are two small examples, and here's another from my last posting just a few years ago.

We were deploying for a weeklong exercise, and as usual, I looked over the housing list I received from the logistics coordinator. I noticed I had been assigned a roommate, but none of the other O-6/Colonel directors had roommates. I called the Major who sent the list, and he said, "Since you're the only female O-6 and the room is big, you'll have an O-5 (lieutenant colonel) for your roommate."

I pointedly asked, "Do any of the male O-6 directors have roommates?" and he said no. I paused to give him a chance to say more, then suggested, "Perhaps I shouldn't have a roommate if none of the other O-6 directors have them." That time, he got my point. I called the O-5, an outstanding officer, and explained, "You won't be my roommate on this trip, not because of who you are, but because when you are the only female O-6, you should get equal treatment and your own room. The standards shouldn't be lowered because there aren't as many of us."

After 27 1/2 years of duty in the Air Force, I retired in northern Virginia. I've been thinking about my leadership style and how I finally mastered work-life balance. I also thought a lot about mentoring, which is now an active part of my life and business.

While some other strong people helped and guided me, I never had a mentor who collaborated with me throughout my career. Many people have given me an à la carte menu of advice and choice tidbits to absorb that have filled my leadership toolbox. At the captain level, I was mentored by several higher officers.

Chuck Milam, the former Acting Deputy Assistant Secretary of Defense for Military Community and Family Policy, helped me get in front of the right people, in the right place, and at the right time to make the difficult jump to full colonel. Although I was running massive programs for DoD, I wasn't physically visible to senior leaders, and this lack of visibility can make it hard to reach the ranks above lieutenant colonel without people like Mr. Milam on your side.

Col. Michael Stough was the 100 Air Refueling Wing Commander when he showed me what exceptional servant leadership looks like. He let leaders lead, and when I made short-sighted decisions, he didn't make me change my decision but instead talked me through it and helped me realize how I could improve my strategic vision and grow as a leader.

Col. J.P. Mickle, my Group Commander at the Transit Center at Manas, showed me how to lead, mentor, and grow a team that feels like a family. He allowed me to make my own decisions as a leader, bounce ideas off him, or discuss proposed ideas and acceptable outcomes. He taught me the value of one-on-one mentorship with your direct reports and reinforced the value of relationships.

While I didn't lead formal mentoring programs at my command, I organized lunches with people of all different grades and led informal discussions about current events and upcoming changes. I made sure I was always approachable, and it was easy to ask me questions. I answered them with courtesy, always. Each Commander who reported to me had a one-on-one with me every week. I taught crafting classes because they allowed me to talk informally with my Airmen. As a woman of faith, I led the women's ministry during my deployments and remote assignments; my faith has always been important to me and has sustained me. There were always programs for men but limited programs for women, so I saw a need and filled it.

After I retired from the Air Force at the end of 2023, I founded Sawdust to Sunflowers LLC, a leadership development, mentoring, and coaching consultancy. I bring every leadership skill I developed into play and help my clients develop their own.

Through guided discussion, I help businesswomen overcome stereotypes so they can effectively communicate and confidently lead in a male-dominated career. *Through my Level-Up Your Leadership in 90-Days* program, leaders learn to increase their leadership confidence, improve communication skills, and avoid costly mistakes that lead to turnover.

I hope to be remembered as the person who successfully reminds others they are not the sum of their mistakes; instead, they're a beautiful work in progress, created to learn and grow through life's ups and downs.

# ABOUT COLONEL TAMMY S. HINSKTON

Born into a career Air Force family, Tammy didn't discover her calling to military service until just months before college graduation. She and her family spent the next 27-plus years traveling the globe, calling wherever the Air Force sent them home.

Upon arrival at her first assignment, her dynamic leadership and resilient personality brought her success. Despite a miscarriage and unfortunate episodes of misogyny and racism, she excelled and received a prized slot to earn her M.S. in Hotel and Restaurant Administration, fast-forwarding her career as a Services Officer. It was one of fifteen educational opportunities she had, including a second Master's degree in National Security and Strategic Studies at the Naval Command and Staff College.

Her 18 assignments and four deployments include almost a dozen years at the Pentagon, where she served the Secretary of Defense and Chairman of the Joint Chiefs of Staff in various high-level positions. She also served as Commander of the Lajes Field, Azores, Portugal plus Morón Air Base, Spain, and as Chief, Services Operations Division for Manpower and Personnel at Headquarters Air Force. She earned 37 medals and awards for her service. In 2021, she had the rare honor of a promotion to Honorary Chief Master Sergeant in recognition of her dedication to serving the enlisted corps.

Tammy's servant leadership style was effective whether she led people or managed a budget and facilities in the United States, Europe, the Middle East, or Central Asia. She vowed there would be no toxic leadership during her watch and encouraged open communications at every level.

After retiring from the Air Force in 2023, Tammy founded Sawdust to Sunflowers LLC, a leadership development, coaching, and mentoring company. She and her husband, EJ, live in Northern Virginia.

# My Legacy of Redemption

## BRAD HAMMOND

I didn't grow up dreaming about boardrooms or business plans. I didn't even know they existed.

I grew up surviving any way I could.

Gangs. Drugs. Hustling. That was my culture. That was my code. I was raised in an urban jungle where respect was everything, and tooth-and-nail survival was the only path. I wasn't handed opportunities on a silver platter—I had to snatch them, even if it meant dancing with the devil.

My truth at the time? The streets were my classroom, and I was a straight-A student in the hustle. A good investment? A pound of weed and a pound of meth.

It took me too long to discover what I thought was my truth, which was my lie.

Looking back, I may have been a crime kingpin on the outside, respected by all I dealt with, but on the inside, I was broken, as broken as anyone you'll meet. I ran a drug empire that earned me power and money, but I had to live with one eye open, never knowing who'd try to take me out next. In that world, your word was your weapon, and any challenge to your name or honor was perceived as a direct threat and needed quick retribution. I could only rely on myself, and I was in a lonely, paranoid, terrifying place. I was an alcoholic for years, as was my girlfriend, finally turning to meth and using the same poison I sold to other addicts. That's about as low as you can get.

A small part of me was still legitimate. I'm an artist, and I turned my art into a very successful, honest tattoo business where I did good work. It could have supported my family well if I had been anyone else. But I was a legend in my own mind, a legend on some very rough streets, and I lived a rock-and-roll star lifestyle beyond what people expected of me.

To support my preferred lifestyle, I built up my drug business. As history shows (and I learned years later), legends built on destruction and threats can't last.

Though I had a family and kids, what most people don't realize is that when you're raised in survival mode, love is a luxury. It was easier to push people away than to risk needing them. I didn't know how to love myself, so how could I receive or give love to or from anyone else?

My upbringing shaped everything. I was born into a world of chaos—gangs, drugs, prostitution, and abuse of every imaginable kind. Survival wasn't a concept; it was a daily decision. Surrounded by criminal influences, I grew up believing the hustle was the only path to power and purpose. I was taught to trust no one, take what I needed, and protect my reputation as a tough guy. My moral compass was shaped by survival—not truth. I didn't know any better. What I now call *dysfunction*, I once called *normal*.

My parents never gave me any love that I could recognize. My mother told me my dad didn't love me; I didn't meet him until I was 16, so I had no way to find out otherwise. I was beaten by my stepfather and step-grandfather almost every day from the time I was a toddler until I said, "no more." When I was 12, I left home and couch-surfed for a year or two, just going home to shower, and then I lived on my own, mainly on the streets. I had my first son at 21 and then three more kids, but I couldn't demonstrate my love for my children or my girlfriend. *Don't show you're vulnerable*, every survival instinct told me.

That type of rough life taught me how to think fast, move fast, and never show fear or allow regrets. But it also created an emotional desert where love, trust, and peace couldn't survive. I chased power, respect, and wealth, even though every gain came with someone else's pain. I missed love, though I couldn't identify it as such.

The streets steal your innocence, imagination, and sense of worth from you. Eventually, everyone you should love is gone, and the relationships are past redemption—but I fought to reclaim that for the last nine years, since I went to prison.

I was one of the lucky ones because I went to prison before I was killed. Now that I'm out on early parole, I speak to teenagers in school about choices and their repercussions. Every time I do, I tell these young men: *"What you're chasing is counterfeit. Respect from fear ain't real. Power without peace is a prison."*

And when I say that, I'm also saying it to the younger me—the kid who thought he had to play God because he didn't believe God saw him.

At the start of this journey, I never thought I'd be where I am today. By sharing my story, I want to show that there's a path to healing and growth beyond your struggles, no matter how terrible or dark your situation is. There's always a brighter future and a better way.

It's *never* too late to live a life of purpose and integrity.

Everything changed when I was sentenced to 50 years in prison.

The prosecutor offered me a five-year sentence, and on my lawyer's advice, I turned it down because the state was dumping charges on me for things I hadn't done. The normal sentence for what I did would be one or two years maximum, and I'd already spent a year in the county jail. The lawyer told me I'd be walking out on the day of the trial. So,

I took my chances on a jury trial—and lost. I had two previous minor convictions and had walked for time served, so I didn't expect much. Up to that point, I honestly thought I could walk away. I didn't expect "three-strikes-and-you're-out-forever." My sentence—50 years!—was longer than most murderers get. At least, thank God, I had never sunk as low as murder, I can tell myself. At the time, though, I thought my sentence was unfair.

I remember sitting in that cold courtroom, every part of me numb. Fifty years. It felt like a death sentence. I decided maybe I should make it one and end it all, and I begged God to take me. But in that dark moment, I heard something deeper than despair, a whisper: "You were made for more."

As it turned out, my sentence didn't end me—it started me, and that whisper became my war cry. First, I accepted that I wasn't done—I was just being rerouted. It was a new chance. I stopped blaming the world and started rebuilding myself from the inside out. I focused on what I could control: my mind, my body, and my spirit. I got sober. I got serious. I became the man I had needed as a child, the man my children required for the rest of their lives.

When I arrived in prison, I finally had the luxury of time and focus for education, and I began to see it *as* a new beginning. Education gave me a new lens, a new language, a new life, and the beginning of a realization that I could do more than be a criminal.

I'd dropped out of school in the ninth grade, and my book learning was nonexistent. I had my art, but no wisdom and knowledge had been passed down from others. Once I was locked up, I opened books and found freedom. I was lucky and could already read well, which isn't the usual case (most prisoners are functionally illiterate). While a prisoner is considered just a two-dimensional criminal, not someone with a future, at least education is available. It's not an easy path, but you can take it.

I earned my GED, became a certified computer repair technician, and worked on my communication and people skills, all the things I wasn't taught and didn't learn as a child. My education in prison taught me to think critically, ask better questions, and envision a different destiny. I studied law, business, history, and psychology. Every page I turned was a brick laid in the foundation of my future. I could see past the streets where I'd spent my entire existence and started plotting a path to a new purpose.

> **" When you're raised in survival mode, love is a luxury. "**

The more I learned, the more I realized how little I knew. Soon, I spent as much time clearing out misconceptions and untruths as I did filling my mind with new facts. The lies I had always believed about myself unraveled. The idea that I was only good for the hustle? Gone. I found worth in wisdom, confidence in knowledge, and healing through understanding.

I met brilliant people in prison, good people who were transformed inside. They helped me go from frustrated to accepting and rewiring my brain. It was hard for me to realize that many of them would never get a chance at freedom—some had undeserved triple life sentences. I made it a point to learn from everyone who had something of value I could learn from, no matter their past or future circumstances.

I also learned about spirituality and religion. Every weekend during the decade I spent inside, I went to church with my friend Tiger, the best dude I ever met there, a God-fearing accountability partner, friend, and hero to me to this day. Prison is not made to change you; you must make that choice. It's a mindset! And you must want it. Prison can either make you mentally strong or break you, and I became strong. I survived.

My art was incredibly helpful in prison. I did a lot of pen-and-ink artwork, portraits for the prisoners and their families, and practiced the barber skills I'd developed, almost a three-dimensional take on tattoos. Above all, I saved the money I got from my work. Tattoos were illegal, or I would have done them too, but I knew I had to be a model prisoner.

Once my remedial education was caught up, I studied investing and learned I had a knack. I studied stocks, trading, and investment strategies and began to master them. By 2019, I'd put together a $25,000 nest egg, hired a financial advisor, gave him some guidelines, including cryptocurrency investments, and let the money accumulate in my brokerage account. By the time I got out five years later, the money had grown by a factor of ten.

I recognize a hustle when I see it, and prison is a professional, big-business hustle. The prison industry makes money on everything by shorting the people they're paid to take care of; they freeze you in winter, cook you in the summer without air conditioning (our cells reached 130 degrees), and feed you inedible swill. The way you're treated can be torturous. In addition, you work for virtually nothing, a few cents per hour. You're a slave. If you don't work, you have no chance of getting parole, and you get in trouble.

Prison has become a big-money machine, a business where prisoners do all the work for free, earning billions for the industries they run. My unit had a mattress factory, and inmates made all the beds for colleges, other prisons, and jails. Other big businesses at my unit were manufacturing license plates, including custom plates, a sign shop, a sticker shop, and computer recovery.

The Texas Department of Corrections collects the money, and none trickles down to better food or conditions, much less pay. As long as life sentences are passed down, TDC will have an endless supply of free labor. In hindsight, it's a genius idea, as long as you're not one of the enslaved people. Of course, they didn't call us enslaved people—we were just criminals.

Though I was one of those guys who worked for free for many years, at least I gained the skill as a computer tech. That's what was important to me then. I had better resources than most and money to help my family. It sure as hell didn't come from the official work I did in prison.

During the pandemic, we were deserted and abandoned. I mean, the officers were terrified of getting close to anyone out of fear for their own health. So, the sick got left to die, the ones who had coronavirus disease (COVID). I watched 11 people die that I knew and had done time with for years, right before my eyes. Medical wouldn't even help them inside; they'd lock them up and isolate them, which in turn led to their deaths. It was so bad at that time. No phones, no mail, no showers, nothing. We were forced to remain in the cells for four months straight. It was painful and scary to think that was how I was going to die in a cell.

My mother passed away at that time as well from COVID-19, which made it that much harder to cope. I was already dealing with a lot. During it all, I had to remain grounded in God, prayer, and a miracle—staying positive and pushing forward. Talk about struggle: Try locking yourself in your bathroom for eight years and then get thrown back into society. Yeah, it's like that.

Prison reform is difficult, but my first improvements would be genuine medical care for those who need it, better food, paying prisoners a livable wage for their work, more structure improvements such as air conditioning, and giving those who have been rehabilitated a chance at life again. I'd also create more programs so fathers can be active fathers from jail. Studies show it would also help keep kids from following their fathers to jail.

Society treats convicted felons like a whole other species, but everybody has made mistakes or done something wrong. It's just important to remember that not everyone is caught. Many who are caught have resources or a good lawyer, and they escape with minor sentences. So many of the men I met in prison shouldn't have been there, and they wouldn't have if they'd had quality legal representation.

Reform needs to start with the sentencing process. Texas gives people a million years for something that should be a six-month sentence. The system is broken, and they have thousands of people never coming home after just minor crimes. I know most people are cynical about people proclaiming their innocence, but there are many innocent people locked up for long sentences.

My cellmate, Julio, had been on parole for 10 years when his wife accused him of domestic violence. There was no evidence, and it was her word against his, but because he was on probation, they accepted her claim that he had pulled a gun on her. I believe him and am sure he did not. Julio was arrested on pure hearsay, and his parole was revoked.

The charge carried a maximum penalty of 20 years, but the sentence guidelines weren't followed. Julio received the equivalent of two life sentences and was returned to prison. I think what occurred was illegal. Because he has no resources to help with the expense of lawyers and investigators, he will spend the rest of his life locked up. With any help, I'm sure he'd be exonerated. It just isn't right.

He's not the only one. There are thousands of prisoners inside in the same boat. If there were a way to investigate our cases, many prisoners would be released or receive sentence reductions, but there isn't. We're on our own. We all had to learn the law the hard way, and most prisoners gave up trying to get out early. Some prisoners don't even have enough money to buy a stamp for a letter to ask for help. You have to be strong-minded to survive and even more strong-minded to come out rehabilitated and not just angry.

Thank God, it was different for me. In my case, prison was the best thing that ever happened to me. That's where I found God, myself, and my vision. That doesn't mean I wanted to stay there for my entire sentence, though!

Unbelievably, I made parole 12 years early, through a fluke. A psychiatrist went to bat for me after interviewing me for a book, and I was one of the lucky ones, with people to vouch for me, money in the bank, a family that wanted me, and a place to go.

The kicker is, when most felons finally get out, after serving their time to society and hopefully being rehabilitated, we're treated as though we'd just done the crime and haven't served our time. We're given $50 and instructions on how to behave on parole.

> It's *never* too late to live a life of purpose and integrity.

Prison reform must include support when the prisoner finishes his sentence and is kicked out with that pathetic $50. You're out, but finding a job is almost impossible. Finding a landlord who will rent to you in today's housing market is even more impossible. These days, the rattiest places want you to fill out paperwork, and if you're without credit or recent job history, without a deposit, without a job or much of one, it is impossible. No one wants to deal with a felon. We're pariahs.

I dream of opening halfway houses, offering a place for newly released prisoners to live, and partnering with places to give them a place to work. All that parolees need are some resources and some support to stay straight and free. Ex-cons also need help catching up with modern life, especially after serving 20 years and not knowing how technology has evolved. Some of these guys, myself included, had no idea how to use an iPhone. I was a computer repair technician, so I wasn't ignorant, but my kids had to set mine up for me. There's so much to learn if you want to do more than exist on the gray edges of society.

People don't know that ex-cons make great employees. We've been working for a few pennies a day if we see the money at all, and if we're allowed to work, we will show up every day and do overtime with a smile. We're incredibly loyal. The need is great; the positive consequences of allowing someone to live like a human being who can be trusted and not feared are tremendous.

Opening halfway houses could be a big part of my legacy, and the repercussions in their families would go on for generations.

Those plans are all in the future. Now, I use what I've learned to empower others. I'm still learning—and now that I've started, I will never stop. I want to inspire those who are struggling.

My passion is art—but my purpose is healing. I've found they can work together.

As a tattoo artist, I've had the honor of turning scars into stories. I've inked survivors, soldiers, celebrities, and everyday warriors. I've seen how a single image can reclaim an identity, rewrite trauma, and restore confidence.

As an autobody modification specialist, I've customized cars that ended up on the pages of magazines, built creative pieces that left people in awe, and collaborated on music videos. One vehicle I made was a hot rod, a 1957 Nomad station wagon that had been sitting in a field for 20 years. It was featured in *Hot Rod Magazine* in 2006 when I was still a teenager. My creativity doesn't have an off switch—it pours out of me in everything I do.

As a pen-and-brush artist, I've healed broken families and reunited them on the page while one member is in prison. I've interpreted old pictures and made the subject alive for the person who desperately needed to see them one more time. In the immediate future, I'm starting a clothing line, beginning with my artwork on T-shirts, and I plan to focus on inspirational art.

But what means the most is using my gifts to serve. Whether mentoring a young artist, creating a memorial tattoo, or just listening to someone's story, I lead with love. I'm willing to tell my story when I think it helps.

I regret the harm I caused to others and myself. I regret believing the streets were my only option. I regret the years and chances lost to crime. I regret the years of parenthood I missed.

But regret is only helpful if it fuels redemption.

What I once used to destroy, I now use to build. I took my street hustle and flipped it into financial literacy. Now, I teach others how to create wealth legally, ethically, and sustainably.

When I hit rock bottom, I realized I had two choices: to sink in shame or rise in responsibility. I chose the climb. My failure became the foundation upon which I built my new life. Failure taught me how to be real, resilient, and lead from the scars, not the spotlight.

The same energy that made me a kingpin now makes me a mentor. I began mentoring others from my cell—writing letters, encouraging them, and speaking the truth. I shifted from being a taker to a teacher. I started setting goals and celebrating small wins. I started believing in the future for me and for those I mentor. I've built businesses, served my community, and spoken on stage. I've turned my regret into a resource.

Success isn't just about reaching the top. I'd reached the top in my first career, and it was a lonely, terrifying place.

Success is about legacy over luxury. I've lived in luxury, and my only legacy was a 50-year sentence.

Success is character over clout. I'm developing my character every day, improving it consciously. I'd been known for my clout, and believe me, it was short-lived. The moment I turned my back, I was vulnerable.

Success means living with purpose, walking in truth, and creating change. It means my children are proud of me—not just for surviving, but for rising. It means giving back to a world I didn't respect and took from.

Success is teaching others to tap into their greatness. It's inspiring a new generation to break cycles and rewrite narratives.

An essential part of my past that had to be fixed was my relationship with my family. Even when I had been present long before I went to prison, I wasn't available to the ones I loved when they needed me.

When I was in prison, being there for my kids physically was impossible; I was just a voice on the phone for them. I preached positivity to them every day for years. I could only imagine the emptiness they felt knowing Daddy wasn't coming home for a long time.

Through it all, I managed to provide for all my children from the inside. I created a team on the outside who worked for me, going to banks and using my power of attorney. I had advisors, lawyers—people who knew what they were doing—who did it for me. I was doing all this from my cell. I'd tell people on my team what moves to make, and we did it. I stayed on the phone like I was running a business inside of the prison walls, building an empire on the outside.

But I could only be there financially. Now I understand what's at least as important is being present in their lives. Our time together is priceless; I cherish every moment with them now, even if we do nothing but sit at home and talk. Just being in their presence keeps me pushing. I'm happy and at peace with them. I live to do what they wanna do. I wanna build them up to continue the generational wealth mission. I don't even want to see them suffer the way I did. I learned the hard way.

I've found that my kids and loved ones are my happy place. Being with them is when I'm most comfortable and at peace. Their struggles have taught me that life is about God, family, love, and building and elevating one another.

My children—Bradley Jr., Kayleigh, Dakotah, and Alexis—are why I breathe and build. I want to give them more than just material things; I want to provide them with tools for a better life. Since I have been given another chance with them, I plan to make the most of it and make up for the years I lost.

This time around, I want to build something that will give them opportunities and new chances of their own and ensure they never have to feel the pain I once experienced. I don't want them to ever consider taking the path I took.

One of the happiest moments of my life was just a few months after I left prison, at a family barbecue. There was no stage, no spotlight, just laughter and love, and my children's faces lit with joy. In that moment, I knew I had done something right—not because I had money or fame, but because I was present.

> " Prison is a professional, big-business hustle. "

We shared stories, danced, and prayed. For the first time, I wasn't thinking about the past; I was embracing the moment. That was success, wealth, and peace.

Years ago, I never would have been able to say *I am proud*…of anything. Now:

- I'm proud of my education.
- I'm proud of my sobriety.
- I'm proud of the relationships I've rebuilt.
- I'm proud of my art, businesses, and mentorship.
- But most of all, I'm proud of the man I've become. I didn't just change—I transformed. I didn't just survive—I resurrected myself.
- My legacy is about redemption, about showing that my past doesn't have to disqualify me. It's about God turning my prison into my platform.
- I want to be remembered as a father, a fighter, a builder, and a giant.
- I want my kids to say, "My dad taught me how to rise."
- I want my community to say, "He gave back more than he took"
- I want young people to say, "If he could do it—I can too"

Because you can.

It all starts within.

And if I can rise, God knows you can too.

So, stand tall.

*You were born to be a giant.*

A big shout-out to you who helped give me a new life:

*Here's a shout-out to the life coaches, field ministers, and all the peer support guys who did time with me and watched my transformation.* I tip my hat to you guys; y'all have your hands full but are doing great things on the inside. I'm proof that what you're doing in the prison is working. We were not all perfect inside, but one thing we did was pray together. That kept me in check; I watched many of you and was inspired and reminded.

*Another shout-out to my best friend Tiger (Clarence Martin).* You showed me what true friendship is. You were there with me in the trenches of the penitentiary through the good, the bad, the fun, and the ugly. And through it all, you taught me to love God and my family. Thank you, Tiger! We've laughed together, we grew together, and it made me a better man. Our friendship is the perfect example of iron sharpening iron because that's precisely what we did.

*And a shout-out to Julio Escamilla, my cellmate of three years,* for signing me up for school without my knowledge. I resented that initially, but I realized God was working through you. That's where my education began, and I never looked back.

*Lastly, here's a shout-out to Larry Wimbrey.* You were a godsend, believing in me like the big brother I never had. You pushed me to be the best version of myself every day for years. I'll never forget the feeling of having your brand of friendship. You always pushed me to be greater—and you are always available.

# ABOUT BRAD HAMMOND

Born into chaos and crime, beaten almost every day by his stepfather and step-grandfather, Brad Hammond survived the only way he thought he could—dropping out and running away. Though literate and articulate, he left school in the ninth grade. He found he had a talent for dealing drugs and became very successful as a local drug kingpin in Fort Worth.

Brad also found a way to work with his artistic talents by becoming a well-known tattoo parlor owner and doing high-end auto body and paint work. He later was commissioned for portraits and other artwork and made money selling his artwork.

By the time he was 29 and the mostly absentee father of four children, he was an alcoholic and meth addict. His third conviction for drug dealing gave him a 50-year prison sentence for a minor drug bust, courtesy of the "three-strikes-and-you're-out" law and the notoriously tough Texas judicial system.

Prison was a life-changer, and Brad realized it offered a remarkable chance for redemption. Brad seized the moment, made the most of the educational opportunities, and learned all he could absorb, including religion. Studying finance, he discovered he had an even better talent for investing than dealing drugs. He invested the money he earned for his art and multiplied it tenfold in six years.

Thanks to a psychiatrist studying him and then vouching for him, he was recently paroled after just a decade in prison. Brad emerged as a sober, productive member of society, and he and his children have been reunited.

His plans include founding businesses, investing, mentoring those needing guidance, and working on prison reform. A key goal is helping newly released convicts find housing and jobs. He speaks to high school students, sharing his story and the lessons he learned the tough way.

Brad and his four children live in Fort Worth, Texas.

 Facebook: Brad Hammond

Hammondempire1

 Hammond_empire1

# Make an Impact With Your Service!

STAN LEWIS

My life has been one of service, whether as a naval officer, a policeman, a mediator with the federal Occupational Safety and Health Administration (OSHA), or through coaching, training, and mentoring teenagers and adults.

Many save their legacy for the conclusion of their story, both literally and figuratively. I firmly disagree with that approach: We must gain a full understanding of our legacy and actively work toward what we wish to leave behind, boldly committing to our path. My legacy will be rooted in the principles of servant leadership and my Christian faith.

I want people to remember me as someone who believed in their innate potential for growth and leadership. My goal is to inspire others to transcend their self-imposed limitations, fostering resilience and self-confidence while reminding them to temper these powerful traits with respect, empathy, and kindness.

Even before achieving my master's degree in organizational leadership, I felt the call of servant leadership resonate within me. It was not an effortless journey; I was committed to honing my ability to serve.

When I left the Navy, I volunteered with the Royal Rangers, a Christian mentorship program I'd joined as a boy. Its goal of evangelizing, empowering, and equipping K-12 boys and young men to be the next generation of Christlike servant leaders is something I fully supported. Though I always showed up, unfortunately I was just going through the motions.

My perspective was transformed when I received a letter from a young man, who wrote, "If not for you and the leaders, I'd have taken my life." I almost broke down when I realized we can truly change lives with even a small amount of communication and caring, and I wondered how much more effective I'd be by being intentional. People are starved for the right kind of help, mentorship, and small gestures of kindness, and many yearn for guidance and connection. Most children will never tell you what they need; someone must show them the way, and hundreds of thousands of them need mentors. I've kept that letter all these years; it's one of my "whys."

But how easily we forget! My own life was profoundly altered by Marvin Lemke, my Royal Rangers leader during my teenage years. He, along with my father, the Reverend Robert L. Hackney, were the two most influential figures in my upbringing, shaping my understanding of what it means to be a man.

I didn't know my biological father, but the Rev. Hackney stepped fully into the role when he married my mother. I was nine years old, and from the beginning there was no "step" to his name—he became Daddy. He was a remarkable person in every way, and he trained me to become a Christian man like himself, someone who cherished his Proverbs 31 wife, who showed kindness and strength in his daily choices. Watching how he loved my mother, and our family, taught me not just to cherish my own wife years later, but to cherish his qualities as a leader who listens and serves.

---

*A Proverbs 31 woman is respected and resourceful with a strong work ethic. She brings honor to her husband, places her family first, and cares for the poor and needy, Robin Revis Puke, Ph.D.*

The Royal Rangers helped to refine me when I reached my teenage years. While it's for boys from both single- and double-parent families, it's a true Godsend to single mothers. My leader, Marvin Lemke, guided my transformation from a typical unfocused teen into a somewhat more useful teenager. He reinforced my father's teachings and served as a guiding light during these formative years. Between the two of them, I couldn't get away with much. Mr. Lemke reminded me that being strong and capable does not exclude being kind and compassionate.

I did fairly well in academics and took part in extracurricular activities in school. I played clarinet in band, participated in basketball and flag football, and served in student government positions, but when I graduated in 1980, I still had a lot of growing up to do.

In college, I spent two years wasting money and not achieving anything while my life went sideways. I dropped out of college to join the Navy, grow up, and see the world. Though Daddy supported my decision, my mother was furious with him for doing so. After the Navy sent me back to college to obtain my degree and a naval commission, I came home after graduation in my summer white uniform. Daddy took one look at me and knew I'd made the right decision. I'd never heard him say, "I told you so" to my mother. Never. But that day he said, "I told you so. That boy needed to go his own way."

As a former college dropout, I had no clue what an immense and important role education would play in the rest of my life, starting almost immediately.

My first two of my eight years in the Navy prepared me to qualify for Broadened Opportunity for Officer Selective Training (BOOST). BOOST was a Navy program designed to help enlisted personnel and qualified civilians become midshipmen working toward a commission as a naval officer. It provided a 12-month preparatory curriculum to improve academic skills, particularly in math, English, and science, along with military training, to prepare individuals for the U.S.

Naval Academy or Naval Reserve Officer Training Corps (NROTC) programs. People told me I couldn't be an officer, that I didn't have the intellect and my race disqualified me. I was determined to succeed; I already knew I was committed to serving and leading, and the path of an officer would help me reach my dream. I just worked harder and developed leadership skills despite the limiting beliefs of others.

When I became a midshipman in 1984, I enrolled at the University of New Mexico on a NROTC scholarship. When I graduated in 1987, I received my B.A. in history and was sworn in as an Ensign. I knew my education had just begun.

As an officer, I learned leadership skills which have served me in every civilian job I've had since. My last duty station was COMNAVBASE Norfolk, Virginia, where I served as the Automated Data Processing Security Coordinator for Rear Admiral Kenneth Carlsen. Unfortunately, debilitating migraine headaches caused me to resign my commission and leave the Navy. I left with a letter of recommendation from Rear Admiral Carlsen. That letter helped me get my first job as a police officer and later as a federal investigator. After leaving the Navy, I filed a disability claim with the Department of Veterans Affairs (VA), but my initial claim was rejected. The rejection hit me hard. I felt an overwhelming sense of defeat and powerlessness and was overwhelmed by negative self-talk. I had totally given into my own limiting beliefs.

One of my key regrets is that I doubted myself and the value of advocating for myself. I was awash in doubt, fear, and uncertainty, questioning my path and wrestling with my limiting belief. I was sure I was a failure. I've since come to recognize that failure is an integral aspect of the journey to success. It served as the starting point for every victory I have achieved.

By leaning into my faith in God, I strengthened my coping skills. During those dark days, my faith became a lifeline—a source of strength that reminded me I was not alone. I also sought the counseling and encouragement of friends and family, whose belief in my capabilities helped shift my mindset from defeatist to resilient.

I realized that resilience involves embracing difficulties head-on rather than allowing them to define me. I had to choose to rise above my setbacks and view them not as the end but as lessons—essential steps in my journey toward growth and fulfillment. Each challenge became an opportunity for self-discovery and reflection, teaching me to adapt and rebuild.

> " Being strong and capable does not exclude being kind and compassionate. "

Twenty years later, the VA validated my claim, and I learned what a powerful skill self-advocacy is. Now I encourage other veterans to avoid the despair I once experienced. I'm a speaker, trainer, coach, and author who has the privilege of helping others navigate their challenges. My own experiences reinforce my strong belief that how we respond to failure ultimately shapes our future and our success.

In 1994, I met my brilliant wife, Barb. God touched my hand after our first date and said, "That's the woman I have for you." Convincing her to marry me was a major achievement, and our wedding was one of the happiest moments in my life. Only my relationship with Christ is more important than my love for Barb. She and I have a wonderful family, our daughter, Aiyana, and son, Rusty.

I served as a police officer for the next 12½ years, including being an environmental investigator focusing on white collar felony offenses. I contributed to the formation of the Illegal Refuse Abatement Team Effort (IRATE), multi-agency environmental group made up of federal, state and county agencies to combat illegal dumping and environmental crimes in Dallas County, Texas. In this capacity, I made presentations to citizen groups, elected officials, schools, and in public meetings. I found I enjoyed speaking and explaining processes, whether technical or not.

In 2005, I was seriously injured in the line of duty while helping to lift a car off a woman. I was ousted from my job when I was hurt, and it was almost 2½ years before my doctor cleared me to return to work. I battled physical pain and uncertainty about my future from Fall 2005 through much of 2007, and Barb was the sole breadwinner in the family. Being let go when I was hurt gave me extra insight into the painful world of those who lose a job because of reporting a workplace injury. Here, too, God was at work, as this experience helped me when I became a mediator helping resolve whistleblower cases with the federal Occupational Safety and Health Administration (OSHA).

I was in my forties when I was injured, and I reassessed not just my career but my entire outlook on life. When I decided to return to college for an M.A., I had a new sense of purpose. Besides, Barb was just wrapping up her MBA and it inspired me to pursue my own graduate degree.

In 2007, the VA finally granted me my first disability rating, and I was able to qualify for a VA Chapter 31 program for disabled vets. I enrolled at Gonzaga University in an online program, and the program paid for my tuition, books, fees, and a new computer. The VA's support reinforced my belief in second chances and the power of education.

Gonzaga University is an elite Jesuit school in Spokane, Washington, with an intellectual approach and a serious academic structure very different than any I'd been exposed to. Jesuits are known for intellectual rigor, critical thinking, and a commitment to service and ethical leadership, and Gonzaga schooled me thoroughly in all of those areas. One of the most important concepts I adopted was the ability to have conversations with people of different faiths, beliefs, and backgrounds without bitterness. Even if we disagreed, we were never disagreeable, we showed respect for each other.

The master's degree in organizational leadership and master's certificate in servant leadership I earned opened doors I'd never considered possible. They weren't merely credentials; they became a means to explore new avenues for leadership and personal growth. I could now delve into servant leadership, a philosophy that echoes my values and approach to coaching and mentoring. I had a new sense of purpose and power that created new opportunities. I had learned to understand leadership dynamics and was empowered with the tools to inspire change in others. I also had the skills to be a peacemaker, which became important in much of my work. It solidified my commitment to lead a life of purpose and service to others.

The day I donned a cap, hood, and gown, and walked across the stage to receive my master's degree in front of my family was one of pride and accomplishment. It proved to me that perseverance truly pays off and can overcome any doubts. It marked not just an endpoint but the opening of new doors, allowing me to step into a future where I could inspire and empower others to pursue their own dreams, just as I had pursued mine. This was a major turning point in my career.

While still working on my M.A., I was able to obtain a position with the U.S. Census Bureau as a Partnership Specialist in January 2008. Later, I was promoted to Senior Tribal Partnership Specialist with the Census Bureau. Here I mentored and led a wonderful team, working with the public at large, tribal governments, congressional staff, state officials, and county and local governments, all with the goal of having an accurate 2010 census.

What I'd learned at Gonzaga about disagreeing without being disagreeable helped me immeasurably in my duties. I traveled throughout Texas, Louisiana, Mississippi, and multiple sovereign tribal reservations developing and nurturing relationships. I treated them as I would want to be treated. Near the end of the 2010 Census, my regional director commented to my supervisor about my work with the tribes, "You know, I believe that this is the first time ever we have no complaints from native American tribes."

In Fall 2010, after the Census and my position ended, I moved to OSHA, first as an investigator, soon becoming a supervisory federal investigator, and then the Alternative Dispute Resolution Coordinator for OSHA Region VI. In this capacity I served as a mediator helping resolve whistleblower cases. Before I retired in 2025, I became one of the top mediators within OSHA.

A mediation is a voluntary form of alternative dispute resolution, where a neutral third party (the mediator) helps two or more individuals or groups find a mutually acceptable solution to their disagreement, helping them avoid the trauma and expense of litigation. The parties involved control the outcome, and the mediator facilitates communication and understanding to help them reach an agreement and avoid litigation.

My experience at OSHA let me see how poorly people communicate. I soon realized in many cases the whistleblower's complaint is merely the visible tip of an iceberg, and a host of underlying communication problems lurk beneath the surface. These complaints often serve as the spark that ignites a much larger fire—a conflagration built on a foundation of unresolved communication issues.

Being a mediator was challenging, rewarding, and every case was different. I cooled the fires and persuaded the parties to work with each other and with me to settle their differences. During my career, I saved companies hundreds of millions of dollars in litigation, preserved jobs, handled 1,262 complaints, closed 796 cases, and had 657 whistleblower settlements.

My work at OSHA kept me busy, right through radiation treatments for cancer in 2017-2018. I had a supportive chain of command that allowed me to work remotely before it became widespread practice in 2020. By this time, I'd become a seasoned mediator, a position that used all the skills I'd developed since my early days as a seaman, including coaching training I received through Maxwell Leadership.

A good coach knows that those they are coaching already have the answer; my job was to help them find that answer. I've also trained other federal investigators at OSHA's training institute on how to do negotiations and bring warring parties into settlement. I love being a peacemaker!

The powers of respect, empathy, vision, and collaboration were incorporated into my work early in my career and have been a major part of it ever since. Tied in with my love for personal development, this ongoing quest for knowledge influences how I engage others in every aspect of my life. I also aim to motivate people to overcome their limiting beliefs, whether they're businessmen or teenagers, and help them uncover their full potential.

> " Failure is an integral aspect of the journey to success. "

As I grew in my skills and my sense of responsibility, my definition of success evolved. When I was young, success was about titles, ranks, and achievements. During my forties, I settled on a somewhat unusual definition for success: The impact I have on the lives of others. I became certified by Maxwell Leadership as a speaker, trainer and coach in 2016, and I began to serve my community with my skill set in many more meaningful ways.

The Royal Rangers ministry has been close to my heart since I was a teen, and I've been an active volunteer adult leader since 1991. The organization has grown from its North Texas roots with its originator, the Rev. Johnnie Barnes, and it's now active in all 50 states and more than 90 countries. Currently, I'm the District Director for the North Texas District Royal Rangers and boys' ministry, a role I never sought but was humbled to accept.

The opportunity to work alongside my mentor and former leader, Marvin Lemke, has been particularly meaningful. Hearing him express his pride in my journey has further reinforced my commitment to service, vision, and compassion. These experiences together reflect not only my personal growth but also the influence of mentorship and the power of community in shaping my path.

Royal Ranger leaders are the sole male influence in the lives of many boys. This is a valuable aspect of the organization. I was in uniform, handing out flyers in church for a camping event, and I noticed a boy being awfully disrespectful to his mother. I asked if I could "borrow" him, and when we had some privacy, I told him quietly, "This is not how a man treats a lady. You need to treat your mother well, not to threaten, ridicule, or disrespect her." He went back to his mother and apologized. She was taken aback and asked, "How did you manage to change his behavior?"

"I spoke to him the way my father always spoke to me—with firmness and guidance," I said.

Weeks later, my staff told me the same young man wasn't going on an upcoming camping trip, and when I asked him why, he said, "I can't go because I don't have a dad or the money for the trip."

"Look around at these Royal Rangers leaders. Looks to me like you have seven or eight dads. And don't worry about the money; we'll find a way," I reassured him. His mother appreciated the help and the guidance, including my gentle but effective reminder about acting respectfully.

Children need someone to show up for them, and they need to be shown the way by good role models, someone they can look up to. They may not ask for this type of help in so many words, but their actions invariably show their need for guidance and mentoring from an adult.

Royal Rangers is equipped to help men mentor boys as servant leaders, allowing them to work side-by-side with their mentees. For example, Royal Rangers uses the shooting sports, such as archery, as a Christian ministry tool; boys love archery, as do I. So much so, I've become both a Level 3 USA Archery coach and a Level 2 Instructor. (I particularly like to shoot compound and Olympic recurve bows). It's a sport with a base of discipline, and one of the few sports in which you can participate all your life.

When I was appointed the District Director for the North Texas District Royal Rangers, I was able to influence a much larger group of adult volunteers, creating a ripple effect of positive change. Except for the years I was in the Navy, and my transition back to Dallas. I've been involved since my early pre-teens—five decades.

Sharing my mission statement and leadership philosophy are common for me to do; I put them in my professional vita and have no qualms about giving them to anyone who is interested. The principles apply to everything I do, whether working at the highest level of professional mediation or working with middle-school boys.

As stated earlier, in 2016 I became a speaker, trainer and certified coach, working with Maxwell Leadership, and to my honor, learning directly from Dr. John C. Maxwell and the Maxwell Leadership team. It was a phenomenal journey and a proud moment when John endorsed me in a side-by-side video.

After my bout with cancer, I began to speak in public more often; it was something I'd been good at and always felt comfortable doing, yet this training brought me to a new level. It helped me with everything I did, both professionally as a mediator and in my ministry, for the next twenty years.

This year I'm in the process of retiring from OSHA, and the extra time that will be created is needed for my focus on Maxwell Leadership and Live2Lead. Live2Lead has had a profound impact on leaders around the globe, inspiring countless individuals to redefine their approach to leadership. Developed by Maxwell Leadership, this event has connected with live audiences and reached over 300 simulcast locations worldwide. Each session is a beacon of inspiration, delivering essential leadership principles that resonate deeply with participants, regardless of their background or experience.

Live2Lead is more than just an event; it is a transformative leader development experience crafted to empower individuals with fresh perspectives, practical tools, and actionable insights. Designed for those eager to enhance their leadership skills, Live2Lead offers attendees the opportunity to learn from world-class leadership experts who share invaluable wisdom and expertise. Participants leave the experience with a renewed passion and commitment, armed with a new action plan to implement in their professional lives.

I've raised scholarship monies for students since 2018 with Live2Lead. This year we're making one major change in the program: We are involving juniors and seniors from local high schools, giving them an opportunity to network with businesses and to benefit from the leadership development training presented by Live2Lead.

I take great pride in my transition into speaking, training, coaching, and mentoring, particularly through my role as owner of Nward Journey. My own Nward Journey has allowed me to share my experiences and insights with others, helping them navigate their challenges while overcoming their limiting excuses.

The most fulfilling aspect of this work is witnessing the transformation in those I train—a shift from self-doubt to newfound confidence and resilience. Each success story stands as a testament to the boundless potential within everyone, and I feel a deep sense of purpose in being part of their journey. Knowing I have inspired others to rise above their limitations and embrace their gifts is an achievement that holds far more significance than any accolade I might receive.

After my service in the Navy, I have always been passionate about personal development and leadership. These interests have shaped every aspect of my life, both guiding my professional journey and enriching my identity. My curiosity and thirst for knowledge have led me to explore a range of subjects, particularly within the realms of leadership, resilience, and personal growth. Reading has been a constant in my life—a cherished hobby that enables me to absorb new ideas and strategies. Through listening to books, taking notes, and reflecting, I have discovered transformative concepts that challenge my thinking and broaden my horizons.

My training experience as a speaker, trainer, and especially a coach has been pivotal to my career as an OSHA mediator. My background equipped me with essential skills that facilitate effective communication and conflict resolution. I have utilized my coaching training by Maxwell Leadership with resounding success in my work as an OSHA mediator, helping to bridge conflicts in hundreds of mediations related to employment law. The unique blend of personal passion and professional expertise has empowered me to play a crucial role in fostering understanding and cooperation during challenging negotiations.

> " Success is the impact I have on the lives of others. "

This ongoing quest for knowledge not only fuels my aspirations but also influences how I engage with others. I am constantly seeking innovative ways to apply what I learn, whether in speaking engagements, training sessions, or mentoring relationships. My love for personal development extends beyond merely consuming information; it inspires me to share insights and facilitate growth in others.

By integrating lessons from my reading and experiences, I aim to motivate individuals to overcome their limiting beliefs and uncover their full potential. I'm now a speaker, trainer, coach, and author who has the privilege of helping others navigate their challenges.

My passion for leadership has cultivated a sense of responsibility to serve my community as a servant leader, which has given me the opportunity to impart the lessons I've learned and the values I hold dear. My commitment to fostering growth and empowerment in others allows me to create a ripple effect of positive change from one leader to another. How I see personal development and leadership from my vantage point aligns with my core beliefs, serving as a guiding force that propels me to help others navigate their paths with confidence and resilience.

Yes, my OSHA chapter is ending, but I look toward the future. I want to see God help me continue to build upon the legacy He has built through me, one firmly rooted in the principles of servant leadership of His Son. I want people to remember me as someone who believed in the inherent capacity for growth and leadership within everyone. God has taught me to push past my limiting beliefs. Now, my hope is to inspire others to push past their limiting beliefs, embrace their unique gifts, and step into their true potential, becoming the best version of themselves.

The teachings and stories I wish to share are meant to encourage individuals to not only seek their own success but to also contribute positively to their communities and uplift the next generation of servant leaders. I envision a legacy where my life story and how God has led and watched over me becomes a source of motivation for others to forge their paths with courage and resilience.

# ABOUT STAN LEWIS

A commitment to service through leadership, mentoring, ministry, and youth engagement defines Stan Lewis's life. Guided by his deep Christian faith, which has shaped his choices since his teenage years, he is devoted to uplifting others. As a young seaman in the U.S. Navy, Stan applied for officer training and achieved the rank of lieutenant junior grade before completing eight years of service.

He served as a police officer for 12½ years, specializing as a white-collar felony investigator. He contributed to the development of the **Illegal Refuse Abatement Team Effort (IRATE)**, a multi-agency environmental task force, and served as a tribal partnership specialist with the U.S. Census. For 15 years, Stan was a federal investigator and served as a supervisory federal investigator focused on claims of retaliation against whistleblowing employees. He was among the top regional mediators with the federal Occupational Safety and Health Administration (OSHA).

Currently, Stan serves as a District Director with Royal Rangers, an activity-based church ministry for boys and young men in kindergarten through 12th grade, dedicated to developing and empowering the next generation of Christlike men and lifelong servant leaders. He now facilitates Live2Lead leadership events, incorporating high school students so they can network with local businesses. Stan works with businesses, organizations, and ministries, developing their leaders as a Maxwell Leadership speaker, trainer, and coach.

Stan's career has been a journey of empowering others through education and skill development, highlighted by his role as a Maxwell Leadership Executive Program Facilitator. As a certified speaker, trainer, and DISC Consultant, he creates impactful training programs to elevate leadership skills and enhance workplace communication.

He earned a B.A. in History from the University of New Mexico and holds an M.A. in Organizational Leadership and a Certificate in Servant Leadership from Gonzaga University.

Stan, his wife Barb, and their two children reside in Waxahachie, Texas.

 www.nwardjourney.com

 Nwardjourney

 nwardjourney

 Stan Lewis, Parenting & Family Coach

 nwardjourney

# Make the Most of the Stage You're On

## MICHAEL CHIASSON

've been privileged to stand on stages across North America for nearly three decades. On some stages, I face corporate executives in plush hotel ballrooms. On others, there are educators and nonprofit leaders in chilly conference halls. The stages I love most are in high school gyms packed with restless students, kids who aren't quite sure why they're there.

Beneath the surface, most people have more questions than answers and far more insecurities than they let on. Whether the person is a chief executive officer (CEO) who's navigating burnout, a parent holding on by a thread, or a teenager who feels invisible, they're looking for basically the same things—connection, hope, clarity, and a reminder that they still matter, and tomorrow is worth showing up for.

Whatever the audience, I have the same goal: To connect with them and interrupt hopelessness.

It's why I begin almost every talk with the same line:

**"I showed up today *not* to get you to believe what I believe or act how I act. My only goal is for us to leave more inspired than when we walked in."**

Those words disarm people, especially those who come in with crossed arms or a cynical sneer. The atmosphere shifts: People stop waiting for the pitch and start listening with their hearts. They accept I'm not there to fix them. I'm only there to remind them what they may have forgotten about themselves (or perhaps never quite believed).

Honestly, I never imagined I'd be on those stages. My parents' marriage ended with a divorce when I was three years old. My mother struggled to find her way, and after several chaotic and dangerous years, she was forced to hand me back to my dad. While he did his best, I often felt duct tape and bubble wrap held my life in place. I didn't have the luxury of thinking about the future; I was trying to survive and get through the day in front of me.

The emotional, physical, and sexual abuse I suffered in my early years honed my survival instincts, and I learned how to read a room, stay alert, and sense when something was off. My hypervigilance became my shield and superpower, and I noticed things other people easily missed. That sensitivity, born from pain and vulnerability, is the most essential tool in my work.

I was skeptical the first time I saw a high school motivational speaker. I slouched in our high school gym, cracking jokes and drowning out the speaker, and I couldn't imagine being inspired. I laughed to myself; what *could this person possibly know about my life that could help me?* (To my surprise, he knew a lot.)

Ironically, I'm now the speaker with the microphone, the one standing where that guy once stood. My absolute respect for the listener stuck with me from my first experience onward. I will never make assumptions about what someone else is going through, so I begin each talk with *the goal of leaving more inspired than when we came in.* With every story I share, I see people in the audience connect, feel seen, and understand that their stories matter. Then, I make it personal by inviting the students to help me understand their lives by sharing their stories with me, and they do. Students have written me thousands of anonymous letters titled *Things We Wish Our Parents Knew: Anonymous Letters from Teenagers That Inspire Courageous Conversations.* That's also the title of the first book I published, one that was years in the making.

Over the years, I've wrestled with the title of *motivational speaker.* I began to reframe and redefine the role for myself. I stared at the word **motivational** until all I could see was the root of the word—***motive.***

Your motive is your reason. It's the "why" behind everything you do. It shapes how you show up, how you lead, how you love, and how you endure. When your motive is clear, your message becomes powerful. And when your motive is rooted in truth and authenticity rather than performance, fear, or ego, it becomes transformational.

Each of us has a motive driving our decisions, relationships, and, most importantly, our view of ourselves. Unfortunately, most of us rarely stop to examine our motives. We distract ourselves to the point of exhaustion. We do everything we can to avoid looking inward. We check the boxes. We build a life that looks good but forget to ask whether it feels true. And somewhere along the way, we lose sight of the masterpieces we were created to be.

Yes, *masterpieces.*

I believe people are not problems to be solved but masterpieces to discover.

And yes, that includes you.

Your masterpiece is not flawless but a living, breathing, evolving work of art, complex and with scars and beauty. When we stop chasing perfection and start reinforcing our unique design—*our* story, *our* pain, *our* identity—we become powerful.

My words aren't judgmental, and I don't have tidy answers. I offer only honesty, humility, and hope. I'm still figuring it out myself, but I've seen enough and lived enough (and failed enough!) to know that radical honesty is the starting line for real change.

We'll focus on three key concepts, and I hope they will help you feel more connected to your true self and more courageous. What matters isn't just what you do but who you become and the lives you affect.

**STEPS:** There's something both simple and profound about a step. Every journey, no matter how long or what kind, begins with just one step.

A step is also one decision, one conversation, or one moment of courage that can change the course of our lives. Too often, we underestimate it and dismiss our small decisions as unimportant unless they produce significant results.

Greatness doesn't come from big, flashy moments. It comes from the thousands of steps we take when no one's watching: the small steps we take toward more responsibility, healing, choosing what's right over what's easy, the steps we take when we're tired, uncertain, or even scared. These are the steps that shape our future.

When I think about my life, my most defining moments weren't when I stood in front of thousands of people, signed a contract to publish a book, or agreed to produce a television show. They were the quiet, internal choices I made long before anyone knew my name, the moments I decided to show up even when I felt I had nothing to give, to forgive when I didn't want to, or to risk embarrassment and rejection when I knew silence was wrong. In short, to do what matters.

When I was a teenager, I was anxious, overwhelmed, and isolated, and I'd convinced myself that no one saw me—not the real me, anyway. Then, one day, a teacher stopped me in the hallway and said, *You are **not** invisible. I see you. And you matter more than you know.*

His thoughtful step gave me enough strength to take the next step and keep moving forward. I have no idea why he was so considerate and generous. He probably doesn't remember taking that step, but I will never forget it.

All of us have a version of these defining "step" moments. They're usually not flashy; they often feel like a whisper of hope in the middle of a hurricane. Yet, when you look at the path of someone who has had a remarkable life, you'll find they've left a trail of small, consistent, often complex steps.

And here's what I've learned: the step itself is more important than its speed. Steps are just daily disciplines and decisions, the internal battles no one else sees.

It's easy to get caught up in comparing our pace with others' accomplishments. When we watch their highlight reels, we wonder why our daily grind feels so unimpressive by comparison and our progress so slow. But growth isn't about impressing anyone; it happens even when we can't see immediate improvement.

> " Every person is not a problem to be solved but a masterpiece to be discovered. "

In my work with students, parents, and professionals, I notice this pattern: *Those who create the most meaningful impact are rarely the loudest, fastest, or most charismatic.* They're the ones who've made peace with the end in mind, who wake up every day and say, "I've not arrived at my destination yet, so today I'm going to give my best and get at least one step closer by the end of the day."

How about you?

- What step do you avoid because it feels too small to matter?
- What step do you know you need to take, but instead, you delay, delay, delay?
- What if the breakthrough you desire most is waiting for your decision to go all-in?

One of the most powerful habits I've built over the years is to ask myself this simple question at the end of every day: *What steps did I take today that my future self will appreciate?*

Some days, the answer is bold: I asked for help. Other days, it's modest: I listened more than I talked. I chose patience and presence over performance.

Over time, these steps create momentum. They shape our character. They become the story we are writing, one paragraph, one sentence, one step at a time.

And remember, not every step needs to be a step forward.

Sometimes, a step back—to rest, to grieve, to reflect—is precisely what we need. These moments can remind us of how far we have come.

Whether you're at a crossroads in your career, have relationship troubles, or maybe wonder if your life still matters, I want you to remember this: All you need to do is take just one step at a time, even when it's slow and complex and even when you doubt anyone else cares.

Every step you take is another step closer to reaching your potential and making your most significant contribution to yourself, your families, and the people you serve.

**CHAPTERS: Life Lessons Measured in Years.** Though *steps* are the daily decisions we make to shape our lives, *chapters* help us understand the broader story we are living. They shape our seasons, help us reflect on life changes, and invite us to notice what we've learned. All too often, we can also see what we've ignored.

For decades, I haven't looked at my life in terms of years but as *chapters*, each one beginning and ending on my birthday. That slight mental shift changed everything. Instead of measuring time only by calendars or accomplishments, I started asking:

- What did this chapter teach me?
- What new and different goals am I working toward?
- How can I describe the difference between the current me and earlier versions in other chapters?

We all live in chapters, whether we realize it or not. Growth defines some chapters; grief defines others. Some are short and intense, like an unexpected loss that rattles your confidence and conviction. Others stretch out slowly, testing your endurance and patience. But if we are willing to accept and learn from the lessons our chapters offer, each one provides invaluable wisdom.

I've selected a few of my chapters to share and explain how these experiences have shaped me.

***Chapter 8*** was a momentous year because my dad got full custody of me. We were just getting used to living together full-time, and I was slowly building my trust after being repeatedly abused by grown-ups.

One day I will never forget is when my dad agreed to take me to the park so I could ride my bike. He tossed my bike into the back of his car, but I didn't notice the wrench he also tossed in.

My training wheels were still on my bike, and I had no intention of taking them off—not me, no way, no how. It didn't matter that I was eight, four years older than anyone else with those wheels, and I didn't even care if my friends or strangers laughed. I wanted to be safe. I *needed* to feel safe.

When we got to the park, Dad took the bike and wrench out of the car and started to remove the training wheels. I panicked and started to hyperventilate. My attempt to plead my case to keep the training wheels was not working. After the intensity of my initial shock at this idea, he calmly said, "Michael, I'll hold on to the bike; I won't let it go. I promise I won't let go until you're ready."

We struck a bargain, and I started pedaling down the walk on just two wheels, Dad holding on to my bike just as he promised. It felt great, despite my fear. After about a hundred yards, I heard his voice in the distance and looked over for Dad—but he wasn't there! He was flat on his back with a broken toe (I later learned), yelling encouragement, "You're doing great!"

Still looking over my shoulder at him, horrified, I did not see the massive oak tree in front of me. The inevitable happened when I turned back to look in front of me. I pedaled head-on into that oak tree, bending my bike, knocking myself half silly, and laid out in the dirt—not my best moment. Dad hobbled up to me and said, "Michael,

I'm so proud of you! You did a great job! You're ready for a big boy bike, and I will buy you a new one."

His support was precisely what I needed in that chapter of my life. It never occurred to him to yell at me for crashing my bike and wrecking it, and it never occurred to me to blame him for letting go, either. My dad chose to focus on what I did right, though it was a short moment. His actions helped me build self-confidence and trust in him, a necessary step in an essential chapter of my life.

That was also the year he gave me the gift of music—my first small guitar. Dad was a fantastic musician who had played with Elvis, Roy Orbison, and others, and music became something we shared. I have played music professionally since I was fourteen and still use it in many events today.

***Chapter 23*** was both a dream come true and filled with terror that it would become a nightmare. I was finally seen and loved for what I did for others and for who I was: the good parts, the not-so-great parts, and everything in between. In my 23rd chapter, I had the privilege of marrying and committing my life to Melissa, the woman whose smile still lightens my life and brings me happiness every moment.

My 23rd chapter also reminds us to live each day with gratitude. Just before the wedding, she was diagnosed with serious cancer that could have killed her. We never take for granted a moment of our more than twenty years together, and she remains healthy.

***Chapter 25*** was one I couldn't have predicted. Life had already taught me that the two greatest gifts we are given are time and people, but then I learned how valuable life can be, no matter how short it is.

When Melissa and I learned (to our surprise) that we were going to be parents, I was nervous about how her body would handle the pregnancy after the cancer treatments she'd gone through. She did develop complications, and we learned our child would probably not make it to full-term. Miraculously, he made it to the 23rd week and was strong enough to fight his way into this world. It was a profound gift that we could hold Jacob for the 24 minutes he lived. We wanted him to know and feel our love more than anything, and we know he did.

Since then, "24" has special significance to us both. Every second we are given is a gift to be experienced and shared. Today, we have been given 24 hours, 1,440 minutes, 86,400 seconds, and the decisions we make today will decide the life we live tomorrow.

***Chapter 40*** was the time I almost lost everything. I was leading a team and raising a family (we now have two beautiful children, Hannah and Simon), and I felt I was failing at both. The impostor syndrome was screaming loud in my head, and I felt my responsibilities were crushing me. Chapter 40 taught me the importance of staying, even when I felt incapable.

> " The self-aware leader will always be the most effective. "

This chapter was and still is painful. I moved forward only because the people who loved and needed me most stayed faithful when others I trusted were no longer by my side.

You have a goal of being a leader and top producer, and you'll inevitably be tested and challenged. Others won't always understand, believe in your ability, or agree with your chosen direction. When you experience this, it'll show you who your tribe is for your next chapter. What helped me tremendously is to remember that people aren't perfect. We are all in the process of becoming our masterpieces, including you and me.

Reflecting on the chapters in your life, you'll find that the process will help you reframe and redefine failure. It adds perspective to pain. And most importantly, it reminds you that your track record for surviving bad days is 100 percent. That's from the day you were born, and you've made it through everyone so far.

That realization alone is worth taking a moment to feel victorious. Where you are today is a miraculous story, and you can celebrate.

First, though, I have a task for you. Take a blank piece of paper and write your current age at the top of the page. Leave room for a title that you'll add later. Write down what this unfinished chapter has taught you, not what you wish you'd learned. Not the polished version. Just the real stuff: the victories, the lessons, the missteps, and the things you never saw coming.

Do you see a theme yet? If so, add the title.

When you have time, go back to a few chapters in your life and do the same for them. You'll more clearly begin to see patterns, themes, wounds, breakthroughs, and moments of redemption you didn't even realize had unfolded.

Here's why it matters: We can't lead, love others, or even live fully unless we understand the stage of life we are experiencing. Too many people think they're still in chapters from the past, reacting to events that happened 5, 10, or even 20 years ago. They're often stuck because they never fully processed the life they were living at the time, and so they don't have the clarity and resilience they need today.

We cannot defeat what we are not willing to define. And what we don't deal with, we're doomed to repeat. Writing the chapters of our story will give us the power to decide what to close and leave behind and what to continue more fully.

Reflection is not a weakness. It's not about navel-gazing or emotional fluff. It's a *strategy*. The most effective leaders I know are the ones who have taken the time to understand their own chapters. They know their triggers. They know who and where they are, and because of that knowledge, they lead with awareness rather than reaction. The self-aware leader will *always* be the most effective.

So, what's the title of your current chapter? Is it *Rebuilding after the Storm*? *Rediscovering Joy*? Maybe it's *Beginning Again (Again)*?

Whatever it is, name it. Own it. Let it teach you through the lessons you have already experienced and are now remembering. Your chapter is still being written, and the best is yet to come.

**STAGES.** These are the moments when we can make our most significant impact.

When I say *stage*, I don't mean a literal platform with lights and a microphone, though yes, that qualifies, too. A stage can be anywhere you are seen, heard, or invited. A stage can be the classroom where you teach, the boardroom where you pitch your ideas, the podcast you launch, your car when you drive your child to school and talk one-on-one with them, or even a hospital room where a friend needs your support.

Stages aren't defined by size or status. Significance defines our chapters.

I've stood on some big stages in my life with thousands of people in the room. It's easy to believe you've arrived when you have cameras and applause. But here's the truth: No big platform-type stage has ever transformed me as much as sitting across from someone broken who just needed to be seen, or when I could give a word of hope to someone who had forgotten their own worth.

Yet many people miss their own stage opportunities because they're too busy chasing someone else's. I've done this, too, when I've missed opportunities to be with my family, even though I know better.

No stage is more important than the one you're on in the presence of your family. The greatest gift they can get isn't a present—it's your presence. When you're making the tough steps and have reflected on your chapter, the stage becomes authentic and impactful; it is not just a platform that compensates for the guilt of your absence.

The greatest stages are the ones where your authenticity speaks louder than your accomplishments.

One moment stands out. I was on a high school speaking tour and had finished a session with hundreds of students. A young man waited until the very end after everyone had cleared out. He walked up to me, eyes low, and said, "I didn't know there was someone who would help me feel I had a reason to keep going." That was it. One sentence. But it held the weight of his world. That was his stage—and mine. No lights, no applause. Just two people willing to be real for a moment.

I've realized that impact is less about impressing people and more about being present with them. We often overestimate the effect of visibility and underestimate the power of vulnerability. Then the question isn't, *How do I get on a bigger stage?* It becomes, *How do I show up fully on the stage I have today?*

Yes, you already have a stage.

It may not feel glamorous. It may not be the one you hoped for. But it is a stage, nonetheless. Someone is watching, listening, and learning from you. Your life speaks to them, even if you haven't said a word.

The people around you are shaped by how you show up and live in your relationships, business, and community. That's the beauty and weight of influence; it's always happening, whether you realize it or not. Being aware and mindful is the game-changer. Recognizing your stage and realizing your influence helps you avoid pretending you have more than you can honestly give.

Certain stages are only accessible and available to those who understand and accept responsibility. If not understood, it will only be a matter of time before that stage becomes the downfall, creating more damage than good.

The stage you have now is exactly where you are meant to be. Showing up on this stage takes courage. It requires risk. It will expose your insecurities. But it will also stretch your ability, deepen your conviction, and connect you to something greater than yourself.

Not because you're perfect. But because you are *willing*.

Here's the great news: Your stage will grow as your purpose and humility grow. You won't need to force it. Just remain faithful to your stage. Keep showing up with integrity. Keep choosing to be courageous. Keep being someone who lifts others higher, not just someone who pretends to look the part.

You don't need a spotlight to be significant; you just need to stretch your comfort zone so the stage grows with you. If your goal for your stage is to expand your natural generosity, your challenge is to first be generous and graceful to the reflection you see in you in the mirror and the ones closest to you, especially children and family. That's anything but selfish in the long run.

Let's analyze some people I've met who stand on incredibly impactful and admirable stages; they're also known for their philanthropy. They have spent their lives and careers working and have become leaders and top producers with all the material trappings of their success. The sacrifices all too many made to reach that pinnacle were at the expense of time with their family.

> " Everybody needs somebody when they feel nobody understands. "

Whatever your stage is, share it with those whom you care for and protect, not just those who will give you recognition and kudos. The plaque or award you receive will only become a meaningless reminder of how great you were to everyone else, except the ones who were your most significant responsibility.

I don't want to scare you; I want to encourage you. We can't change the past or the things we've already done. We can, however, change what we do now and in the future.

Ask yourself:

- What stage am I currently standing on?
- Am I fully present there or waiting for a better stage?
- Would I enjoy my stage as much if I were anonymous?
- Have I brought those closest to me onto my stage?

I hope you choose to own your stage, whether it's for five people or 5,000. Realize that the power of what you bring to the world doesn't depend on how loud your voice or how big your audience is, but on the authenticity and motive of your message.

With every step, we become stronger; in every chapter, we become wiser; and in every stage, we become braver.

Faith is at the center of my life.

Faith guides me through every decision I make and every difficulty I face. Faith is my motive and reason for my work, and whatever success may come, I see my ability as a gift entrusted to me. Whatever good I have accomplished was built on two platforms. The first helps fuel what I love. My company serves many organizations through keynote presentations, executive team development, and print and video resources. You can learn more at *followmc.com*.

What I feel most honored and privileged to do is through the work of a Canadian registered charity Melissa and I founded in 2009. We serve all types of school communities in North America for students and parents through live events and online resources. Our mission, *inspiring the world one student at a time,* is critically important, especially today.

Let's take the time to reiterate: You are not a problem to be solved—you are a masterpiece waiting to be discovered.

That masterpiece is not found in perfection, applause, or hustle—it's revealed in the steps you take every day. It's recorded in the chapters you've lived and the one you are currently living–honest, messy, and brave. It's displayed on the stages where your truth, ability, and experience meet someone's needs.

So, go! One step at a time. Turn the page. Make the most of the stage you're on. And in whatever industry you choose to offer the masterpiece of your gift and talent, I am confident that anyone who has the privilege to work alongside you will be better and able to shine brighter because of you.

# ABOUT MICHAEL CHIASSON

Michael is a charismatic public speaker, musician, and author, whose career spans more than twenty-five years in the U.S. and Canada. Every year his compelling and personal approach inspires almost 50,000 students, parents, teachers, business executives, and others across North America.

His goal is to inspire hope in those he reaches, reminding them that their track record for getting through every hard day has a 100% success rate.

A professional musician since he was 14, he is known to create unique and memorable experiences for his audiences through multiple senses. As the visionary behind the **Chiasson Group** and founder of **Access 52**, a Canadian registered charity, Michael champions the belief that people thrive when they have a clear vision of who they are, what they're capable of, and how they can make their greatest contribution.

Michael authored *Things We Wish Our Parents Knew*, published in 2025. Written for parents, the book draws from tens of thousands of anonymous letters written to Michael by students he's met over the years.

Raised by a single parent in Houston, Texas, he was a cynical, restless teenager and survivor of abuse when he met his first inspirational speaker. He never forgot the positive impact the speaker made on him. In September 2000, Michael moved to Canada to attend college, earning a diploma in leadership and sacred studies. Ever since, he has continued developing his skills as a musician and communicator.

Michael believes two of our greatest gifts are time and people, and he treasures his time with his wife, Melissa, and their two children, Hannah and Simon. They live on the prairies of Alberta, Canada.

 access52.com

 Michael Chiasson

 @michaelchiasson